CASE
STUDIES
AND **CASE-BASED**
LEARNING

T0386577

CASE
STUDIES
AND CASE-BASED
LEARNING

TODD STANLEY

Routledge
Taylor & Francis Group

NEW YORK AND LONDON

First published in 2019 by Prufrock Press Inc.

Published in 2021 by Routledge
605 Third Avenue, New York, NY 10017
2 Park Square, Milton Park, Abingdon, Oxon OX14 4RN

Routledge is an imprint of the Taylor & Francis Group, an informa business.

Copyright © 2019 by Taylor & Francis Group

Cover and layout design by Micah Benson

Library of Congress Control Number:2019908468

ISBN: 978-1-0321-4344-6 (hbk)
ISBN: 978-1-6182-1885-8 (pbk)

DOI: 10.4324/9781003233428

TABLE OF CONTENTS

INTRODUCTION

As a social studies teacher for many years, one of my all-time favorite quotes to discuss with students was "History repeats itself." I know that this saying is more fortune cookie fodder than ground-breaking assertion, but, time and time again, this proclamation has rung true. The Greek Empire fell when it spread itself too wide and it was unable to govern such a large territory, causing the empire to splinter. Lo and behold, a little while later the Roman Empire grew too large, fragmented, and crumbled. There are other obvious examples:

■ the Industrial Revolution and the Computer Revolution,
■ the assassinations of Abraham Lincoln and John F. Kennedy,
■ World War I and World War II,
■ the civil rights movement and the LGBTQ rights movement,
■ the fact that I keep telling the car rental place that I will take the insurance even though my wife reminds me I should not.

1

DOI: 10.4324/9781003233428-1

We learn from the past—both successes and failures—throughout our lives. The first time we burn ourselves with fire or a hot pan as a child, we know the next time to keep our hands away. The numerous mistakes we during young adulthood are lessons that we take into the future. We make mistakes and learn from them so that we do not repeat them. When you think of some of the greatest lessons you have learned in your life, they most likely stem from a great success or a mistake that either set you straight or changed your approach to a problem or task.

Imagine this, however. What if you could learn from someone else's mistake . . . or success? In the classroom, this is where case studies and case-based learning come into play. Case-based learning involves looking at and learning from past events and situations, using another's mistakes or successes as an educational tool. Consider the possibilities in the classroom. Students will see not only the value in the corrected version of the case, but also the value of any mistakes because there would be no lesson without them. They can also see what has worked before and then try to repeat the success.

The question becomes: Why don't we just study the successes? Why would we want students to look at someone's failure? The answer is that accepting mistakes is a life skill we do not do a good job of teaching in our public schools. We tend to reward success with gold stars, stickers, or nice shiny A's. Mistakes, however, are chastised and punished. If you do not believe me, take a look at the way we grade most student work. We begin with 100% and then whittle away at that total with each mistake that is made. Say you forgot to capitalize consistently in your paper; that lowers your grade to a B. If you miss an order of operation when completing a math problem, it deducts from your total score. In the traditional classroom, we are teaching students that it is not okay to make a mistake.

Case-based learning allows students to see the value in making mistakes. Instilling the notion that there is value in mistakes will translate to students' lives when they are out in the real world, making mistakes and learning from them. This is why case-based learning can be so transformative in the classroom. We can actually show students what learning from mistakes looks like. Once you take away the fear of failure, students are going to be more willing to take risks, and with these risks come high rewards of learning.

Case-based learning does not just have to involve events that have already happened; it can also involve events that are currently happening or might happen. For instance, consider global warming. Students could certainly study past cases of how global warming has affected the world, but you could also ask students to tackle the problem as it stands today. What actions do we need to take in order to slow down or remediate the effects of climate change? What are we currently doing, and is it effective? We can also try to anticipate what dealing with this case might look like in the future. With the rate of global warming and the increase in our planet's temperature, how may we have to adjust the way we are living? Rising temperatures can affect agriculture, melting of the ice caps, rising oceans, ecosystems, etc. Students could analyze solutions other scientists have developed to anticipate these problems and even make a case for a solution of their own, using existing research to back up their decisions.

To build your understanding of case studies and case-based learning, this book is organized into three parts. Part I defines what case-based learning is, discusses the advantages of using case studies in the classroom, and describes the valuable skills that can be learned by students through case-based learning. Part II shows you how to develop your own case studies and implement case-based learning in your classroom. This section includes the steps to writing your own case, how to train your students for case-based learning, and what your role as the teacher looks like in the case-based learning environment. Finally, Part III includes examples of case-based learning for each of the four core content areas—language arts, math, science, and social studies.

By the end of this book, you will see the value in using case-based learning strategies with your students and begin to implement cases during your lessons. One of the biggest challenges in writing this book was that case-based learning is not as widely used as its cousins, project-based learning or problem-based learning. Because of this, there is not a ton of resources out there for teachers to pull from. If after reading this book you are bold enough to create your own case and would be willing to share it, I will create a repository at https://www.thegiftedguy.com, where the cases can be found so people can download these resources for free, giving the creator full credit for his or her work.

PART I

WHY CASE STUDIES AND CASE-BASED LEARNING?

DOI: 10.4324/9781003233428-2

CHAPTER 1

WHAT IS CASE-BASED LEARNING?

Case-based learning is commonly used in the medical and law fields. Throughout medical and law school classes, young men and women studying to become doctors and lawyers study past cases to identify ways to improve health care or legal arguments. By doing so, they can become more knowledgeable and effective in their professions.

For example, Ignaz Semmelweis, a doctor in the mid-1800s, began to look at past cases of women who gave birth and, specifically, those who died of childbed fever (Zoltan, 2019). He looked at the cases of women who gave birth in a ward at a hospital that was staffed by all male doctors and medical students, and another ward that was staffed by female midwives. He found that women who gave birth in the ward staffed with doctors were 5 times more likely to die than those in the midwives' ward. At first, he believed this was because women in the doctors' ward gave birth on their backs

DOI: 10.4324/9781003233428-3

while those in the midwives' ward gave birth on their sides. He began having everyone instruct mothers to give birth on their sides, but there was no change. Then he noticed that when a woman died in the doctors' ward, a priest would walk through the room ringing a bell in honor of the dead. He came to the conclusion that this ringing was literally scaring women to death. He was wrong again.

When one of the doctors died from childbed fever, Semmelweis realized the illness did not just affect women giving birth. He looked at other differences in the ways the two wards operated and noticed that the doctors performed autopsies while the midwives did not. Eventually, he surmised that the increase in deaths was caused by the doctors' hygiene. After performing autopsies on the bodies of the deceased, the doctors would then deliver a baby, infecting the mother. The solution, then, was simple—they needed to wash their hands (Zoltan, 2019).

We see handwashing and hygiene as obvious necessities nowadays, as there have been many studies on how infection is passed. But, at the time, the concept was revolutionary to the point that many people discounted Semmelweis's claims. Disgraced, he later died in a mental institution, but his findings eventually led to massive changes. Once doctors began to wash their hands more regularly, the number of deaths from childbed fever dropped dramatically. If Semmelweis had not carefully studied past and present cases at his hospital, however, we may have never learned the importance of simple hygiene practices. More than that, Semmelweis failed a few times, learning what did not work through trial and error of additional cases. He was able to look at several cases and test hypotheses until he found a correlation.

Like Semmelweis, today's medical students study past cases for research purposes and to improve patient care. Similarly, lawyers spend a considerable amount of time looking at past cases so that they can try to determine a precedent for future cases. The staff of the Princeton Review (2019) described what courses first-year law school students should expect to take:

- **Torts:** Studying the rationale behind judgments in civil cases.
- **Contracts:** Studying past court cases to follow the laws governing the conditions and obligations contracts represent.
- **Civil procedure:** Studying past cases that govern who can sue whom, how, when, and where.
- **Property:** Studying the laws governing the purchase, possession, and sale of property in the U.S.
- **Criminal law:** Studying past and hypothetical cases in a class that relies heavily on Socratic dialogue.
- **Constitutional law:** Studying issues of government structure and individual rights.
- **Legal methods:** Studying fundamental skills in legal research, analysis, and writing.

You will notice a lot of instances in which students will have to read, analyze, or write about past cases in an effort to learn how to be a lawyer. And this continues throughout their career, as they look at past cases to establish precedent or to determine how to proceed in their own cases.

There are even sports and games that rely on past cases. Chess is one that comes to mind. Those who study chess seriously often analyze past chess matches. The games of Garry Kasparov, Bobby Fischer, or Mikhail Tal can often improve your own game if you study the strategies they employed, the traps they set, and the ways they developed their pieces, as well as the mistakes they made. Football is another. Coaches study videos of past games to determine tendencies and patterns of other teams that they can exploit, or to build strategies that can lead to their success.

How do we translate case-based learning to the classroom? How do we implement these strategies in our classes? First, we must know what case-based learning in the classroom looks like.

DEFINING CASE-BASED LEARNING

Case-based learning (CBL) is defined as:

> a teaching method which requires students to actively participate in real or hypothetical problem situations, reflecting the kinds of experiences naturally encountered in the discipline under study. (Ertmer & Russell, 1995, p. 24)

Case-based learning asks students to analyze something that has already occurred and try to develop a better solution. In science class, this might involve looking at cases that scientists have encountered and exploring what they did in certain situations. Students might try to replicate an experiment, with opportunities to divert from it or to try to change variables in an effort to improve upon it. Rather than simply reading about science in a book, students actually practice science like real-life scientists. Taking part in a virtual lab, working with real data, or conducting a simulation can inspire students to use inquiry to solve an authentic problem. For example, consider the *Unusual Mortality Events* simulation in which students try to determine the cause of the 2013 high death rates of manatees, brown pelicans, and bottlenose dolphins (Nova Education, 2015). Rather than simply following the previous experiment step by step, students develop their own research questions and hypotheses, pursue their own testing strategy, and make independent final conclusions.

In math class, case-based learning might involve looking at someone's mistake in attempting to solve a problem, analyzing it step by step, and determining where he or she went wrong, taking the correct action, and solving the rest of the problem. This is authentic because it shows students how to approach a solution should they be working on a problem and encounter a similar situation. This shows students how math is not just about the end results but rather the process one goes through while trying to get a solution. If students can learn to do this, they can apply it to any sort of problem. They know which mistakes to check for and what pitfalls may exist.

In language arts, students might look at the actions of a character in a story and juxtapose how events could have been different had that character taken a different course of action. For instance, in *The Scarlet Letter*, the main character, Hester Prynne, decides not to reveal who the father is of the baby born out of wedlock. As a result she is forced to wear a scarlet letter, branding her an adulterer. What might have happened if she had told the people that it was the town minister, Dimmesdale? Would the consequences have been different? Would Dimmesdale have lived, and would he and Hester have been able raise their daughter together? Although this is a fictional book that takes place nearly 400 years ago, this ethical dilemma is timeless. People are forced to make similar decisions every day, always dealing with the notion that there are different consequences for different actions. This could certainly spark a lot of debate and inquiry, as well as show students that different decisions can result in different consequences, giving them pause when they are making such decisions in their own lives.

In social studies, students might study an event like President Truman's decision to drop the atomic bomb in Hiroshima, analyze if it was the right decision, and try to predict what might have happened had this event not occurred. Because history repeats itself, students can analyze the decision-making process as well as the outcome to inform future decisions, such as how the United States will deal with North Korea should it continue to develop arms.

There are all sorts of ways you can use case-based learning in the classroom to build inquiry and bridge what students are learning from theory into practice. A case study can even involve a court case. When studying impactful court cases, you can bring them to life and make them even more authentic by having the class participate in a mock trial in which students take their analysis and research and put it into practice. This allows them to not only read and understand the significance of the case, but also experience it. Students find themselves in the shoes of those who made major decisions, leading to more feelings of empathy toward those decision makers and building real-world relevance.

Lundeberg (as cited in National Research Council [NRC], 2011) defined case-based learning with even more detail:

> Cases involve an authentic portrayal of a person(s) in a complex situation(s) constructed for particular pedagogical purposes. Two features are essential: interactions involving explanations, and challenges to student thinking. Interactions involving explanations could occur among student teams, the instructor and a class; among distant colleagues; or students constructing interpretations in a multimedia environment. Cases may challenge students' thinking in many ways, e.g., applying concepts to a real-life situation; connecting concepts [and/or] interdisciplinary ideas; examining a situation from multiple perspectives; reflecting on how one approaches or solves a problem; making decisions; designing projects; considering ethical dimensions of situations. (p. 29)

A couple of important terms are used here, including the word *authentic*. Case-based learning should be authentic by its very nature.

The target of students' study in a case-based learning experience should be a real-life situation that they will greatly benefit from analyzing. The second important term used is *challenge*. We often throw this word around in the educational world as though you can simply wave your magic wand and—poof—students are challenged. *Challenge* also often serves as an inadequate answer to the problem of what we should do with some of our brighter students and those identified as gifted. The usual answer is that we should simply challenge these students more. The issue is that there is often little guidance for how to accomplish this. There are those teachers who challenging students just comes naturally to; they are able to constantly push students to get them to dig a little deeper. The probing questions that emanate from these teachers' own curiosity get students to think more critically. This skill can be developed, however. Just because it is not a part of your teaching arsenal currently does not mean you cannot begin to use it in your classroom. Like anything we do as teachers, you will try and fail, try and fail a little less, and try until you succeed. The important thing is that you try. Just because challenging students does not come naturally to you does not mean it should be ignored. Developing higher level thinking questions is a good way to challenge students and will definitely come into play during the CBL process.

The crucial concepts to unpack in Lundeberg's (as cited in NRC, 2011) definition are:

1. interactions in which students must turn their thought processes into an explanation, and
2. challenges to student thinking.

Both of these greatly inform your classroom role and the actions you will want to take while students work on a case.

Case-based learning falls under the umbrella of inquiry-based learning. Thus, there can sometimes be some overlap between case-based learning and problem-based learning. The major difference between these two modes of learning is the amount of guidance provided by the teacher. In problem-based learning, the teacher typically opts for a completely hands-off approach, allowing students to figure out everything for themselves, including what research to look at and how to plan and control their progress on the work. There is also little to no preparation before students begin trying to solve the problem. There is simply more structure to case-based learning, and this structure is very purposeful. This structure acts as the scaffolding for the learning, enabling students to achieve at higher levels. The idea is to provide structure that allows students access to the next level of thinking and then push them to the next level by challenging them to consider things they have not. Because of this aspect, the teacher's role is much more active than with problem-based learning. The teacher needs to be more cognizant of using guiding questions to make students think more deeply and offering immediate feedback. A lot of the learning takes place through these conversations. The teacher must be ready to provide a space and time for these conversations to occur so that learning goals can be best met.

STEPS TO CBL

Because case-based learning involves more structure than other inquiry-based strategies, it is important to go through all of the steps in order to maximize the learning that takes place. Although there are variations to these steps, here are the more common ones (Williams, 2005):

1. **Case is presented:** This is an introduction to the case that is usually provided by the teacher.
2. **Case is analyzed by the group:** The small group begins to analyze the case. Students determine what they already know, as well as what new information they will have to

find in order to be successful. You can actually do this as an entire class if you so desire. The important thing is that students are the ones generating ideas.

3. **Ideas are brainstormed:** The group collaborates to determine an approach to the case.

4. **Group formulates learning objectives:** Through their approach, students determine what they are going to learn throughout the process. These become learning objectives that can be assessed once the results are shared.

5. **Group sorts the research:** Students combine what they already knew with what they learned together to try to create a product that encompasses their solution.

6. **Findings are presented:** The results of the case study are shared with either peers, parents, a panel of experts, or some other public forum.

7. **Students reflect:** This is where a lot of the learning will come because students will reflect on not only the end results, but also the process they took to get there.

Throughout these steps are plenty of opportunities for you to be involved and ask questions that will not only drive the action of the learning (the students can do that for themselves), but also deepen the conversation. See Figure 1 for a graphical representation of the process. The brackets represent prime opportunities for you to be involved in the conversation.

Teacher involvement in the process is discussed in far greater detail in Chapter 6, but, generally, you should interject to inspire students to think about something in a different way or to wonder "What if?" For example, if students are developing learning objectives that are merely scratching the surface and not diving deeper into the topic, you might make suggestions for a way to introduce controversy to the case. Let us say that students are looking at a science case involving cloning. Students might come up with learning objectives such as:

- Is cloning scientifically possible with today's technology?
- What are ways cloning could be used to benefit society?
- What are some reasons people are opposed to cloning?

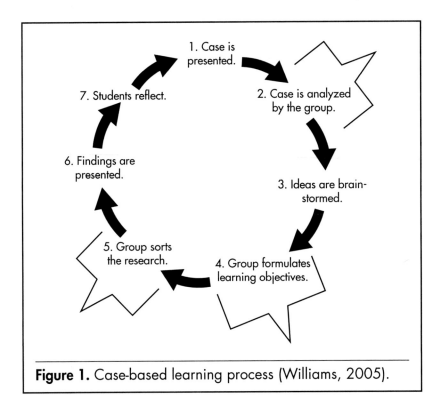

Figure 1. Case-based learning process (Williams, 2005).

These are student-appropriate learning objectives that will no doubt allow students to gain a basic understanding of the multifaceted issues concerning cloning. You, however, might suggest some questions to extend students' thinking:

- What if a couple lost their young child and used cloning to produce another child?
- Could organs be harvested using clones to replace damaged ones?

These more ethical issues bring a lot more to the table in regard to thought and exploration of the topic.

Keep in mind that the teacher's main goal in case-based learning is not to control the learning but rather to nudge it in interesting directions. The students are still doing the bulk of the work, but your position is not as laidback as the problem-based learning environment. You still need to be involved as an impartial observer who seeks to challenge the easy way out as well as continually raise the bar.

WHAT A CASE STUDY MIGHT LOOK LIKE

To be clear about what a case looks like, let us run through one. This is a case involving a lesson for a teacher. It could be used with students studying to get their education degree or with younger students who want to learn more about what goes into teaching a lesson.

1. Case Is Presented

This following case would be given to students to look over. They could do this prior to coming to class, or you could set some time aside in class to allow them to read it individually. Then, you would decide how you are going to break them into groups to study the case:

> Tom is an eighth-grade teacher who is developing a lesson about rocks. He decides that he is going to have the students work in groups throughout

the lesson. He divides his students into groups of five, alphabetically, until he has six groups. He decides he is going to have students research different types of rocks to learn the three types—metamorphic, igneous, and sedimentary. After a couple of days during which the students are engaged in research, Tom receives the following information in an e-mail from a parent: "Mr. Thomas, my son is not getting along with his group."

As part of the assignment, after conducting its research, each group must create a poster that defines the three different types of rocks. Each group is provided with poster board and a package of markers. A couple of days into students' poster creation, Tom gets a phone call from another parent. This parent's daughter is complaining that she is having to do all of the work in her group and that there are members of her group who are not doing anything.

Finally, students must develop a presentation in which they find an example of a metamorphic, igneous, and sedimentary rock around their neighborhood and explain how they know which type of rock it is. During one of the presentations, the group has an igneous example and a metamorphic one, but when prompted for the sedimentary example, one of the group members shrugs his shoulders and Tom grades the presentation accordingly.

The lesson is graded using a rubric. Tom checks the appropriate boxes, tallies a holistic letter grade, and gives the rubric back to each group before moving on to the next lesson.

2. Case Is Analyzed by the Group

Following the presentation of the case, the case would be analyzed by the group. The group's goal would be to identify possible problems/issues in the case. Students might recognize some obvious issues, such as:

- student grouping,
- parent communication,
- group work, and
- grading practices.

As the teacher, you would want to listen to these conversations and lead students into looking at some deeper issues, such as:

- classroom environment,
- group dynamics, and
- creation of objective rubrics.

Once the group has settled on a few problems, students should begin developing solutions.

3. Ideas Are Brainstormed

Considering the number of possible problems/issues to study, the group can decide to tackle them in teams or to work on all of them together. Remind students of a potential trickledown effect: Solving one problem may lead to a resolution of other problems. Take, for example, the issues with student grouping and the group work. If the group studying this case decided to tackle group dynamics, this might end up taking care of the other issues as well. If there is an overall environment established for groups, there may not be a problem with the way groups are determined. The group studying the case could develop numerous solutions to the same problem and bring them all to the table when the group begins to formulate learning objectives.

4. Group Formulates Learning Objectives

After the group has brainstormed solutions, its next step would be to formulate learning objectives. It is important to prioritize these problems, to determine what order they should be solved in and which ones to devote more attention to. There were a lot of issues with this particular case, but by prioritizing them, students will begin to get at the root of the overall problem. They might take the case and create three learning objectives:

> From studying this case, we will learn:
> - how to set up project work for better student engagement,
> - how to objectively evaluate a performance assessment, and
> - how to be proactive with parent communication.

These are strong learning objectives because they can be researched easily and many different strategies are available in the literature to address them. They are also realistic because they can be solved. Throughout any case, the teacher will want to make sure that students are attempting to address feasible learning objectives. Consider the challenges if the group had come up with this learning objective instead: "We will learn how to stop students bickering with one another in groups." This might be really difficult to solve. Students are probably going to bicker with one another at some point or another, especially when working in groups. There is no stopping that, but there are strategies that can be employed that would help to handle this situation. A better way to phrase the learning objective would be: "We will learn how to create an environment for good group dynamics." This would be more realistic, and students could find research and theory in order to support the solution.

5. Group Sorts the Research

Once the learning objectives are set, students would seek to provide research-based solutions to these problems. This could involve articles, interviews with teachers, and other resources that could inform this course of action. From this, students would propose a new strategy for how the case should be handled. For instance, when it comes to how to objectively evaluate performance assessments, students might come across research on the value of well-written rubrics or find a video seminar on how to write such rubrics. Students would take these theories and put them into the practice of their own case, writing a comprehensive rubric for the lesson concerning the three different types of rocks. Students would create authentic solutions to the problems based on the facts and details of the case.

6. Findings Are Presented

These solutions would be shared with the class and, ideally, to an authentic evaluator. In this particular scenario, having three or four teachers serve on a panel to evaluate the solutions the group presents would be a good way to provide an authentic assessment. Alternatively, students could present to the school board and/or the superintendent. Presenting to an authentic audience further enforces the theory-to-practice nature of case-based learning and provides students with real-world application, further legitimizing and increasing the value of their work. Typically, a performance assessment such as this would be graded using a well-written rubric.

7. Students Reflect

Reflection is probably the most overlooked step in the learning process. Often, students learn a lesson, apply it to something such as an assessment, and then move on to the next lesson after demonstrating mastery. Many classrooms do not provide students with the space or guidance to reflect upon what they have truly learned. Content standards and learning objectives aside, students have their own takeaways from a lesson. Those takeaways may be different than what the teacher expects. Regardless, it is important for students to understand what they took away from a lesson.

In our case example, providing students with a reflection prompt would get the ball rolling toward some meaningful reflection. Students could be provided with a prompt such as this: "After working on this case, do you think the act of creating a lesson is easier, more difficult, or about what you thought it to be?" Here students could reflect using their experiences from the case, as well as the lessons they have experienced throughout their lives. This prompt could be used in a few ways, such as by having students write in a journal, pair and share their thoughts with another classmate, or take part in a class discussion. In this particular case, students could be asked to write an educational blog for an audience of other teachers. Through writing a blog post, students can be more informal with their writing style and more honest with their thoughts than through writing a formal paper or report. These blog posts could be submitted to teacher journals or collected on a website run by the teacher. These authentic avenues mean students' work would be seen not just by the class, but also by a real-world audience.

MAKING A CASE

Case-based learning is "a means of participatory and dialogical teaching and learning by group discussion of actual events" (Dunne & Brooks, 2004, p. 9). According to the Gwenna Moss Centre for Teaching and Learning (2017), case-based learning experiences can be implemented through:

- written cases,
- video cases,
- interactive cases,
- simulations,
- games, and
- field trips (para. 2).

No matter the format, the teacher has a very different role than in the traditional classroom. A teacher's main goal is to provide thought-provoking content, as well as ask probing questions that require students to dig a little deeper.

The next chapter dives into the advantages of case-based learning.

CHAPTER 2

ADVANTAGES OF CASE-BASED LEARNING

You can probably already see some of the natural advantages to using case-based learning, but you might not be aware of all of them. Some of these advantages include the following (Barrows & Tamblyn, 1980; Mullins, 1994):

- Students sort out factual data, apply analytic tools, articulate issues, reflect on their relevant experiences, and draw conclusions they can relate to new situations.
- Cases add meaning by providing students with the opportunity to see theory in practice.
- Students are required to utilize self-study to consolidate learning that occurred in groups.
- Case-based learning requires integration of prior and newly acquired knowledge.
- Students engage in inquiry and the development of support provision for their conclusions.

DOI: 10.4324/9781003233428-4

- Students seem more engaged, interested, and involved in the class.
- Because many cases are based on contemporary or realistic problems, the use of cases in the classroom makes subject matter more relevant.
- Students develop crucial learning skills.

The most impactful classroom advantage, however, is the opportunity for students to see theory become practice. The reason that this is so important is that students spend much of their school years learning a lot of theory. They learn how to solve a math problem but not how that math presents itself in the real world. Or students are given the rules for grammar but do not produce anything that is seen by anyone outside of the classroom. This theory-based education can be frustrating because students do not learn the context of any material. These lessons exist within the vacuum of the classroom, and their real-world application may not be visible for students. Any chance you get to show this pathway to students will greatly benefit them. Through real-world application, students see the finished puzzle rather than a single piece. They are going to understand how their learning fits into the big picture of the world around them.

That is why case-based learning is such an effective teaching strategy to use with students. There will be many times in their lives when they will be able to look at a case presented to them and use the skills acquired through this process in order to make a better -informed decision. They do not have to end up being a doctor or a lawyer in order for this to be pertinent. Cases present themselves in other forms as well. There are many opportunities in our lives to learn from the past. Case-based learning makes learning so much more authentic because it employs skills students will actually be able to use. Even though this is a long-term benefit, the short-term advantage is that because case-based learning is more relevant, students are more likely to be engaged in their studies. Being engaged makes it so much easier for students to gain an enduring understanding of the lesson at hand. As Bruner (as cited in Center for Innovation in Teaching and Learning, 2019) pointed out, the case method:

> Models the process of inductive learning-from-experience: It is valuable in promoting life-long learning. It also promotes more effective contextual learning and long-term retention. (para. 3)

CONNECTIONS TO BLOOM'S TAXONOMY

A major advantage of case-based learning is that by going through the various steps of a case, students will encounter all levels of Bloom's (1956) taxonomy. Bloom's taxonomy covers six levels of thinking:

- **Understanding:** Involves recognizing or remembering facts, terms, basic concepts, or answers without necessarily understanding what they mean.
- **Comprehending:** Involves demonstrating understanding of facts and ideas by organizing, comparing, translating, interpreting, giving descriptions, and stating the main ideas.
- **Applying:** Involves using acquired knowledge—solving problems in new situations by applying acquired knowledge, facts, techniques, and rules. Learners should be able to use prior knowledge to solve problems and identify connections and relationships, and how they apply in new situations.

- **Analyzing:** Involves examining and breaking information into component parts, determining how the parts relate to one another, identifying motives or causes, making inferences, and finding evidence to support generalizations.
- **Creating:** Involves putting elements together to form a coherent whole or reorganizing into a new pattern or structure.
- **Evaluating:** Involves presenting and defending opinions by making judgments about information, the validity of ideas, or quality of work based on a set of criteria.

These levels of thinking coincide with the natural progression of working on a case. In each one of these steps (Williams, 2005), students will use one or more levels of Bloom's taxonomy in order to accomplish their goals:

1. **Case is presented:** Students will use the understanding and comprehending levels of Bloom's taxonomy to gain an understanding of the situation. This part typically involves the students reading information about the case in an effort to understand what they are going to try to accomplish. They will have to use their knowledge to put the case into terms they can comprehend in order to gain an understanding of the case.
2. **Case is analyzed by the group:** Students engage in the analyzing level of Bloom's taxonomy. The group begins to break down the case into parts that can be investigated in more depth. Part of this involves students determining what they already know and, most importantly, what they will need to find out in order to be successful.
3. **Ideas are brainstormed:** This step involves a combination of several different levels of Bloom's taxonomy, including understanding, comprehending, and applying, as the group builds off of its understanding of the case to begin brainstorming ideas, and analyzing, evaluating, and creating as the students determine how to address the case.

4. **Group formulates learning objectives:** Students engage in the applying level of Bloom's taxonomy as they determine how they are going to apply what they have learned in the form of learning objectives. Students use their new knowledge to try to solve a problem, identifying connections and relationships.

5. **Group sorts the research:** Students engage in the creating level of Bloom's taxonomy in order to determine how to combine old and new information together to create a product that encompasses their solution.

6. **Findings are presented:** Students engage in the applying level of Bloom's taxonomy to show what they have learned, utilizing their learning objectives to help others understand.

7. **Students reflect:** Students engage with the evaluating level of Bloom's taxonomy and reflect on what they learned throughout this process.

The connections between case-based learning and Bloom's (1956) taxonomy allow students to gain a basic understanding of a topic and then be able to take that understanding to another level, whether it be applying, analyzing, or evaluating. These upper levels of Bloom's taxonomy—analyzing, creating, and evaluating—require students to think at higher levels, using skills such as critical thinking and creative problem solving, and allow students to make judgments, providing them with ownership of their learning.

In many traditional classrooms, students only access the lower levels of understanding and comprehending. They memorize content long enough to apply it to a test, and then often forget it. Using the higher levels of thinking leads to an enduring understanding. This is another huge benefit of case-based learning.

CONNECTIONS TO THE ENGINEERING DESIGN PROCESS

Case-based learning can also engage students in the engineering design process (Engineering is Elementary 2019; see Figure 2). This five-step cycle (ask, imagine, plan, create, improve) is the same process real-world engineers utilize. After a case is presented, students must *ask* questions to help them better understand the topic. This questioning carries over into the brainstorming process, during which students *imagine* solutions to their case. Once students have brainstormed many possible ideas, they must choose an idea and *plan* how to execute it. The creation comes in the product aspect. Here students must be able to clearly communicate their solution to the case through what they *create*. An authentic audience can up the ante and make students more accountable. The *improve* phase happens mostly in the reflection part of case-based learning. As part of the reflection, students should think about what they could have done better or what could have improved the case. Teachers might even work a little bit of improvement into the presentation of findings by carving out a little class time for students to practice and make their presentation better. The teacher might also make observations during other steps of the process and ask questions that cause students to pause and think about how what they are working on could be better. Table 1 outlines connections between case-based learning and the engineering design process.

Why is employing the engineering design process such an advantage? Because it provides the following benefits. Students (MESA, n.d.):

- Learn to work together by creating and designing a plan;

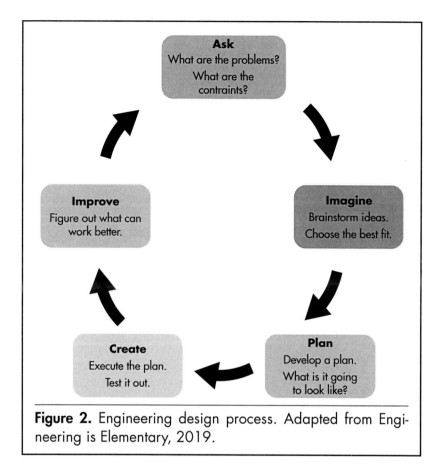

Figure 2. Engineering design process. Adapted from Engineering is Elementary, 2019.

- Describe and justify a plan, learn to share and present their thoughts, justify answers, debate/defend/explain their thinking;
- Solve problems by finding answers to questions;
- Collect data, analyze data, make modifications and adaptations;
- Justify why they make changes, state opinion, remedy solution;
- Become self-learners;
- Learn through trial and error and from mistakes; and
- Learn to revise ideas, making and testing predictions. (para. 1)

Table 1

Connections Between CBL and the Engineering Design Process

Case-Based Learning Process (Adapted From Williams, 2005)	Engineering Design Process (Engineering is Elementary, 2019)
Case is presented.	
Case is analyzed by the group.	Ask: Students analyze the case's problems and constraints.
Ideas are brainstormed.	Imagine: Students brainstorm possible ideas and choose the one that would be the best fit.
Group formulates learning objectives.	
Group sorts the research.	Plan: Students take the idea/solution they have chosen and develop a plan for execution.
Findings are presented.	Create: Students execute and present their plan, determining what will work through testing.
Students reflect.	Improve: Students take what they have learned in the create phase and see if they can develop a better solution.

You will notice that a lot of these advantages of the engineering design process echo the benefits of case-based learning in general, showing how well the two can work together.

THE VALUE OF CASE-BASED LEARNING TO THE STAKEHOLDERS

Case-based learning can be an effective method for keeping classroom morale high for the stakeholders, namely the students and the teacher. In a review of the effectiveness of CBL in health profession education, Thistlethwaite et al. (2012) found that:

- students enjoyed the method and thought it enhanced their learning,
- instructors liked how CBL engaged students in learning, and
- CBL seemed to facilitate small-group learning.

No matter what method of teaching the teacher employs in the classroom, it will not work if students and the teacher do not believe it is helping the learning process. Case-based learning creates a different environment than the traditional classroom. This different environment increases student engagement. When students step into the case-based learning classroom, they know it will not be like all of the others. There is going to be something different; thus, they will have to stay on their toes. Because there are so few classrooms using case-based learning, the CBL classroom is going to stand out from the others. Add to this the authentic nature of CBL with its connections to the real world, and students cannot help but be engaged.

In CBL, because the role of the teacher shifts to friendly interloper rather than the showrunner, the teacher is going to be more engaged as well. The traditional teacher is a showrunner, meaning he or she has to be in charge of everything, making sure everyone is paying attention to the learning, not necessarily engaged in it. This role tends to be based on compliance, not engagement. This role puts the cart before the horse and leads to teachers thinking that because students are compliant, they have the opportunity to be engaged. This overlooks the fact that if you simply engage students in learning, they will be compliant. They will not need an overseer making sure they are doing what they are supposed to. They will be engaged because they are interested in what they are learning—a win-win for the student and the teacher.

CHALLENGES IN CASE-BASED LEARNING

It would be misleading to assume that there are only benefits to participating in case-based learning. The strategy, like all teaching strategies, comes with its own set of challenges. Some of these are laid out by Mostert (2007):

- **Unfamiliarity with case teaching:** Many students are used to the traditional form of teaching involving lecture and passive learning. Case-based learning is anything but passive. In order to get the most from it, students must be willing to actively participate in both discussion and reflection. This is a skill some students might not possess because of the drill-and-kill nature of many classes, so it might take some training to get your students ready for the type of learning in CBL.
- **Case preparation:** Setting up the case can be quite time-consuming for the teacher. He or she has to find the appropriate research to match the level of his or her students. Not only that, the teacher has to anticipate what sort of issues

might come up in the discussion so as to be ready to push students to the next level. There is a fair amount of preparation on the side of the students as well. Students typically have to read the case prior to coming to class to discuss it and should take copious notes that reflect their understanding as well as insights. Students not used to this strategy will have a bit of a learning curve.

- **Case emphases:** Because the role of the teacher is so different than would be considered typical, there are nuances that can be tricky to understand. Some of these nuances involve figuring out what issues to emphasize in the case. If it is a good case, the students can take it in all sorts of different directions. Helping students to navigate a case and pointing them in the direction where the most enlightenment might occur, especially given the lack of others who could model such a strategy, can make the adjustment for the teacher quite a learning experience.

- **Speculation:** Although we want students to think outside of the box regarding a case, it can be challenging to make sure students are staying within the realistic limits of the case. If the case is written properly, there are facts and details which cannot be altered, meaning the solution that students develop must exist within the context of the case as it is presented. Too much speculation can be counterproductive to the learning process, and teachers have to learn how to help students interpret without compromising the learning objectives of the case.

- **Case complexity:** The main strength of case-based learning is its ability to allow students to go into great depth. Unfortunately, this can take a bit of time to uncover, and some of the finer issues might be overlooked. Teachers have to be able to lead students to unpack these deeper issues.

- **Participation in case discussion:** A lot of the learning comes in the conversations that students have with themselves and the teacher. The deeper and more rich the conversation, the better the learning is going to be. Of course, this only works if the students are willing and able to discuss. If you have students or groups who do not actively participate, it is going to be difficult for them to gain insight.

- **Group work:** The dreaded "g" word can sometimes be a student and teacher's worst nightmare. Getting students to work together in a fair manner can certainly be quite a juggling act, but if the group is able to pull it off, the rewards are far greater than any risks. Students might need some training in what working in a group looks like and what their expected role might be.

Regardless of these challenges, a teacher who is dedicated to making CBL work in his or her classroom is going to reap the benefits. There are going to be a lot of growing pains, and there will be times when you feel it would just be so much easier to go back to the traditional way of teaching. But like anything, with time will come understanding and comfort, and from this, a classroom environment in which students are learning on a completely different level than their peers in other classes. This is the prize you must set your eyes on. After all, CBL is about the students and helping them to become lifelong learners.

MAKING A CASE

Although there are many specific benefits to case-based learning, there are a few overall benefits. These are:

To *provide students with a relevant opportunity to see theory in practice.* Real world or authentic contexts expose students to viewpoints from multiple sources and see why people may want different outcomes. Students can also see how a decision will impact different participants, both positively and negatively.

To *require students to analyze data in order to reach a conclusion.* Since many assignments are open-ended, students can practice choosing appropriate analytic techniques as well. Instructors who use case-based learning say that their students are more engaged, interested, and involved in the class.

To *develop analytic, communicative and collaborative skills along with content knowledge.* In their effort to find solutions and reach decisions through discussion, students sort out factual data, apply analytic tools, articulate issues, reflect on their relevant experiences, and draw conclusions they can relate to new situations. In the process, they acquire substantive knowledge and develop analytic, collaborative, and communication skills. (Centre for Teaching and Learning, n.d., para. 3–5)

These benefits make the use of this teaching strategy well worthwhile. Case-based learning can be a big undertaking and require the role of the teacher to shift from being in front of the class to being a part of the class. This can be a challenging transition for some, but the overall benefits easily outweigh any minor hardships the teacher must deal with in learning how to use this exciting and engaging method of teaching in the classroom. Like anything, the more you use it, the more familiar and comfortable you will become.

CHAPTER 3

HOW IS CASE-BASED LEARNING AUTHENTIC?

If there is one benefit that stands above the rest, it would certainly be the fact that CBL is authentic in nature. Case-based learning (Reeves, Herrington, & Oliver, 2002):

1. has real-world relevance;
2. is ill-defined, requiring students to define tasks and sub-tasks needed to complete the activity;
3. comprises complex tasks to be investigated by students over a sustained period of time;
4. provides the opportunity for students to examine the task from different perspectives, using a variety of resources;
5. provides the opportunity to collaborate;
6. provides the opportunity to reflect;
7. can be integrated and applied across different subject areas and lead beyond domain-specific contents;
8. is seamlessly integrated with assessment;
9. creates polished products valuable in their own right rather than as a preparation for something else; and
10. allows competing solutions and a diversity of outcomes (p. 564).

DOI: 10.4324/9781003233428-5

In other words, by engaging in CBL, students will develop skills, such as problem solving, collaboration, time management, and task prioritization, that they can put into play when they venture out into the real world to find a job. How many students sit in lectures and take notes or read textbooks as part of their jobs? If the answer is very few, then why are we still teaching students using these methods? We should be using methods that teach so much more than content. CBL teaches students how to think and how to learn.

CASE-BASED LEARNING IS AUTHENTICALLY MESSY

Even though cases cannot be put into a nicely organized bundle and disseminated like prepackaged lessons, that is sort of their charm. Cases are messy, which is what makes them authentic because life is messy. Studying cases can (Schommer, 1990):

1. demonstrate the sometimes unexpected ways in which different factors interact;
2. help students learn how to negotiate in a complex world and recognize, anticipate, and work around variables; and
3. help students understand that the structure of knowledge can be complex, not always simple.

Case-based learning falls under the umbrella of authentic learning (see Figure 3). At the top of the figure is inquiry, which has students driving the learning. With the idea of collaboration at its forefront, inquiry learning branches off into several different teaching strategies. Two of these are the more well-known project-based

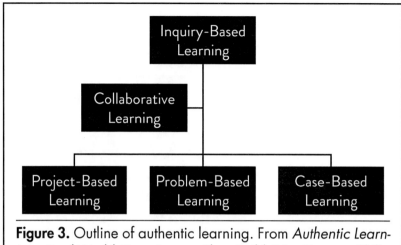

Figure 3. Outline of authentic learning. From *Authentic Learning: Real-World Experiences That Build 21st-Century Skills*, by T. Stanley, 2018, Waco, Taylor & Francis. Copyright 2018 by Taylor & Francis. Reprinted with permission.

learning and problem-based learning. If you walk into any school in the country, you are bound to stumble across an educator who is using one of these methods to engage students.

Case-based learning, however, is less common. You would be hard-pressed to go into a middle school in the United States and find it being used. You might see it more commonly used in places such as Australia, Canada, Japan, and Europe. One place you are likely to see CBL in the United States is at the university level. Harvard has a long history of using case-based learning, beginning in 1870 when it realized that the basic lecture format was not giving students the chance to practice what they were learning at the law school. The business school followed suit nearly 50 years later, creating cases built around actual business issues and decisions that had yet to be made. The medical school finally implemented case-based learning in 1985, seeing the value in tutorials and active learning as opposed to lectures (Garvin, 2003).

The logical question is: Why are we not using case-based learning more commonly in the U.S. in primary and, especially, secondary schools? After all, case-based learning is an authentic way for our students to learn. Why would teachers not want to utilize this strategy to ensure the benefits that come with it?

BENEFITS OF AN AUTHENTIC EDUCATION

Case-based learning is authentic because it bridges the gap between theory and practice. Students actually get to see for themselves how what they are learning fits into the context of the real world. The logical question then becomes: What makes an authentic learning experience so great? There are several benefits to learning authentically. Authentic learning:

- encourages students to assimilate and connect unfamiliar knowledge;
- exposes students to different settings, activities, and perspectives;
- enhances transferability and application of theoretical knowledge to the real world;
- creates opportunities for students to collaborate, produce polished products, and practice skills (e.g., problem solving);
- builds students' capacity to exercise professional judgments (Curtin Learning and Teaching, 2015, sec. 2).

You can clearly see the overlap between case-based learning and its authentic nature because:

- **Authentic learning boosts motivation.** Students have a natural drive to learn from the world that they are living in

42

and are motivated to understand, interact with, and even change the world.

- **Students learn better in authentic learning environment.** Students learn by making use of real tools with real purposes to make real products.
- **Authentic learning prepares students for future careers.** Students need to understand the global economy. Thus, students should be provided with context for their learning and learn to solve problems using different information sources as if they are in the real world.
- **Authentic learning makes concepts easier to be assimilated.** It is easier for students to learn when they are encouraged to investigate a topic on a personal level.
- **Authentic learning blends theories with practice.** Students can be forgetful if they do not apply the knowledge that they learn from time to time. With exposure to new contexts, application of the concepts in new settings and participation in assorted learning activities, students can better retain content (Har, 2013, pp. 2–4).

Cases are about something that already has or is currently happening in the world. As a result, it is important to make the process of working on a case, including the assessment of what was learned, as authentic as possible. Part of that authenticity is found in having students use skills that they will be using not just in school, but also when they are beyond its walls and making life decisions. Authentic learning builds skills that transcend the classroom and will benefit students no matter what they decide to do in life.

21ST-CENTURY SKILLS AND CASE-BASED LEARNING

Wagner (2008) introduced the following seven survival skills in his book *The Global Achievement Gap*:

- critical thinking and problem solving,
- collaboration across networks,
- agility and adaptability,
- initiative and entrepreneurship,
- effective oral and written communication,
- accessing and analyzing information, and
- curiosity and imagination.

Wagner (2008) developed this list of skills after talking to many global business leaders who identified these as in-demand skills in the workplace. Business leaders felt that they were not seeing a lot of qualified workers because schools were not preparing students in these skills. Wagner (2012) discussed a mismatch between schools focusing on material that can be easily tested instead of teaching skills that are needed for success in the 21st-century workplace. Wagner described the difference between how schools teach and are run as opposed to what is going to best prepare our students to compete in a worldwide marketplace (as cited in Vander Ark, 2013):

1. The culture of learning is about individual assessment and sorting, but innovation is a team sport;
2. The culture of schooling is compartmentalized, but innovation happens at the boundary between disciplines;
3. Most schools exhibit a culture of infantilization and passivity; by contrast innovators are active creators;

4. The culture of school rewards risk aversion and penalizes failure; the culture of innovation demands risk and iteration; and

5. Schools rely on extrinsic motivation, innovators are usually motivated intrinsically. (para 5)

The easy fix here is simple; teach the survival skills to students. This is not a difficult decision to make; there are not a lot of barriers. Survival skills can still be taught even if you are adhering to the content standards. The survival skills are not taught in the content of a course, but rather through the style of teaching and learning the teacher chooses to employ. Schools can sometimes dictate a lot of policy for teachers, including content, books, assessments, computer programs, and other curriculum. One thing they usually do not dictate is the way the teacher is going to teach his or her students. Teachers, for the most part, have the ability to decide the strategies they are going to use in the classroom. When you walk into a classroom and the teacher is standing at the front of the class, talking at the students in a very traditional manner, administration did not force him or her to choose this. This style of teaching tends to be very passive. Because it is passive, students are not active in their own learning and are unable to develop 21st-century skills. How can students learn to be creative when the teacher is dictating the product? Can students figure out how to adapt when material is presented in just one manner? Is it possible for students to take initiative when the teacher is not providing them with opportunities to do so because assignments are closed-ended? There are, of course, exceptions, but when students are passive, so is their learning.

Twenty-first century skills are also not limited by subject area. Collaboration can be taught in a math class, problem solving in a language arts class, effective written communication in a gym class. These are choices made by the teachers in how they deliver their content. You may not get to choose the what, where, when, who, or why in your classroom, but you can choose the how. Know that you have that power, and you can choose strategies that allow you to better teach the survival skills our students would greatly benefit from. The more active your students are, the more actively they are learning.

The reason why authentic learning strategies, such as case-based learning, should be used regularly in our schools is because of the way they are set up. Students learn these survival skills in a very organic manner. It is not like they are doing a unit on creative thinking or taking a test to show how much initiative they have. These skills are woven into case-based learning seamlessly, naturally occurring as the case unfolds. Students, at times, are not even aware they are learning these skills. They are simple working on their case and, in the process of doing so, are building these survival skills and creating a tool box they will be able to access later when needed.

HOW SURVIVAL SKILLS PRESENT THEMSELVES DURING A CASE

Let us walk through a case and see how it utilizes each of the seven survival skills Wagner (2008) outlined. The case involves housing issues and air pollution in Mexico City. These are both fairly large problems by themselves. If you are working with a younger class or a class that is just being introduced to case-based learning, you might want to just focus on one of the problems. For the purposes of this example, however, we will look at both.

To start the case, a group of four students is given several articles dealing with the housing problems in Mexico City. The students find out information, such as how Mexico City is home to

22 million people, how it covers 3,700 square miles, and how more than half of the homes and buildings constructed are done so without regulations (Ireland, 2015). More troubling is that at the center of the city lies the D.F., where 9 million residents live in 16 boroughs across 570 square miles. Within these tight quarters pass more than 3 million vehicles a day, almost half of them 20 years or older. The exhaust of so many outdated cars in such a small area has created an air pollution problem.

By finding out all of this information and sifting through what is and isn't important to the case, students employ the skill of accessing and analyzing information. The students then take the information they have researched and must develop possible solutions for both problems (housing and pollution). This is going to involve much curiosity and imagination. Obviously if the solution was a simple one, someone would have come up with it already. Because of this, the solution must be one that is outside the box. This will involve a combination of research and curiosity and imagination. The students come up with several possible solutions for each problem:

Housing:
- Organizations such as Habitat for Humanity
- Building affordable but sustainable housing
- Having more people to enforce regulations for homes
- Using ADUs—small houses that fit within existing homes
- Implementing cohousing where each family has a private home with shared common spaces

Pollution:
- Implementing a car-driving ban
- Regulation of car emissions
- Introducing air purifiers/scrubbers
- Offering affordable but newer cars
- Improving the public transit system

Some of these solutions are going to be too outside of the box and thus unrealistic to implement. Others are going to be too expensive or might require too much oversight in order to be successful. The students need to find the one that is the best fit possible. This will require critical thinking and problem solving skills in order to develop a solution that is both feasible and innovative. If students settle on a solution, then there will be further research needed to determine how the solution works, how it will be implemented, how it would be paid for, and the expectations for how long until Mexico City residents see change. If the students decide to tackle the pollution problem by creating a public transit system, they would have to research many different examples and look at additional case studies to see how it has been implemented in other countries. Mexico has already tried some options with moderate success. The country has a day-without-a-car program 2 days a week, as well as a rapid transit bus system. However, these have not solved the problem of vehicles being in such a tight space. Given the congestion of vehicles in the D.F., what if a public transit system could be put into place that does not interfere with traffic? An option would be to create a public transit system like the one in Bolivia, which has an aerial cable car system where the transport is suspended above the ground, meaning it would not cause congestion. Students could research how La Paz set up its Mi Teleférico in phases, as well as how it has rolled out different lines over time (MacGregor, 2015). This may serve as a basis for the solution in Mexico City. During this phase of the case, students would also have to use the skill of agility and adaptability. They would not be able to copy Bolivia's plan, but rather adapt it to fit their own needs. Students can take lots of different ideas and combine them to make something new as well. If they decide to develop a system for building affordable but sustainable housing, they might find all sorts of possible products out there. There is hemp concrete that can be used to construct homes, and recyclable materials such as shipping containers can be turned in housing.

The group settles on houses built using 3-D printers. The printers will dramatically reduce construction and labor costs, allowing the city to repurpose old construction materials, such as concrete, clay, or mud, and print each house for under $5,000. The 3-D printers require no wages and no rest periods and can produce identical designs in a short timeframe. They can also switch to new designs with a few clicks of a computer mouse. The students research how 3-D printers have been used in Singapore, where three dorm-style buildings have been constructed using existing "Prefabricated Pre-Finished Volumetric Construction" methods (Nield, 2016). At this stage, the students employ adaptability in regard to the technology. The students consider whether there are better 3-D printer systems now available that could be utilized to improve the quality of the construction or the building efficiency. They also begin to wonder: Are there countries other than Singapore that have employed this idea with success? How can 3-D-printed homes be better made?

This case is not a simple matter of finding the easiest, most obvious solution. This case is about being innovative and thinking a little differently than what might lead to the typical solution. Taking on these bold ideas requires students to show initiative. This may involve additional research, talking to experts, running tests, and all sorts of activities that will make their solution better. Because students are engaged and care more about what they are learning, getting them to show initiative will be much easier. Throughout CBL, student groups are also usually competing against one another to try to determine the best possible solution. This, too, acts as motivation because the group that presents the best idea more than likely will be the one that took the most initiative, which is how the real world works. Initiative also comes into play because students are involved in inquiry learning. They are the ones making decisions and assigning roles, not the teacher. A student who waits around to be told what to do is not going to perform well in a case. Students who take it upon themselves to figure out things without the guidance of the teacher will be the most successful.

Typically a case involves a product that shows what students have learned. This could be anything from a presentation, to a mock trial, to a podcast, or a paper. Because the nature of the case is authentic, it is important to try to find an authentic audience for the product. If students are looking at a case that involves the theory of evolution, can they present to an audience of scientists from the local university? If students are looking at the collapse of Enron as a major company, could the audience be a group of businessmen? If the case involves a mock trial, can you find a lawyer to be the judge? Regardless of who the audience is, the students will have to show effective oral communication in order to convey the solution they have developed. The fact that the audience is authentic just raises the bar that much higher because students are not presenting to peers, but to experts. That means they are really going to have to know their stuff.

Even if there is not an oral aspect to the case, students are going to have to communicate their solution somehow. It could be in written communication through the creation of a website, a brief they have created, or a business plan they have developed. This written communication has to be clear and has to show the reader what this solution would look like. Without a clear communication of the solution either through oral or written means, or both, you are not going to see what students learned. What was the process students had to go through in order to arrive at their solution? Many times this is where the learning takes place.

In our Mexico City case, students will have to develop both an oral and a written communication to convey their solution. The students must deliver an oral presentation to a panel of urban planning graduate students from a nearby university. Students will have 10 minutes to present their case to the panel. Afterward, the panel will choose the solution that seems most realistic, viable, and innovative. Because the presentation is only 10 minutes, there are a lot of details and ideas that students may not be able to share. The students will show the rest of their solution through the creation of a step-by-step plan that shows how they are going to roll out their changes and development. Students will be given requirements for the plan, and the panel of experts will be able to look through students' plans to answer any questions they might have about the solution.

The final survival skill has been used throughout the entire case. This is the skill of collaboration. Because students work in groups in order to develop their solution, they have to find effective ways to work together and be productive. This means debating, compromising, taking on specific roles, and learning to create something much better as a group than could have been created by any one individual. There may have been specific roles in the case, such as splitting the team in two and having one focus on the pollution problem while the other looked at the housing, or there might have been a project manager who was overseeing the entire solution while other group members focused on very specific tasks.

Collaboration skills are so important that there is an entire chapter devoted to their development later in the book. Students are not given a lot of training on how to work effectively in groups. Yet, when we thrust them into the real world, students are often in situations that require them to collaborate with others. A person who lacks collaboration skills is going to have a very tough time in the adult world. Collaboration is crucial at work, in family life, and even throughout leisure time. Because of this, collaboration is probably one of the most powerful skills that is taught through the use of case-based learning.

MAKING A CASE

The world is changing quickly. The day and age of someone going to work for a company for 30 years and then retiring with a gold watch is a thing of the past. The average worker stays at his or her job for 4.2 years before moving on to another, switching jobs an average of 12 times during his or her career (Doyle, 2019). And this is not always a lateral move within the same industry. Some people are switching careers altogether, entering into an entirely new field.

When you think about this from a schooling point of view, one wonders how you can get students prepared for such a job, considering they might be switching it in a few years. Add to this the fact that many jobs in fast-growing industries did not exist 10 years ago. That means that schools need to prepare students for jobs that have not been created yet. Not only that, many of the vocational jobs we used to prepare students for are becoming obsolete due to technology. We need to have a means to make our students viable without narrowing their options. We need to be teaching our students universal skills that will translate into any profession. We also need to be making their learning as authentic as possible so that they are prepared for this ever-changing world. Case-based learning will help with both of those monumental but important tasks.

PART II

PUTTING IT ALL TOGETHER

DOI: 10.4324/9781003233428-6

CHAPTER 4

HOW TO WRITE YOUR OWN CASE

There are several examples of case studies provided in this book (see Part III for more), but they might not fit your grade level or cover the curriculum you are required to teach. You may have fallen in love with case-based learning and want to do more of it in your classroom. There are examples of cases online. Ideally, you should create a case yourself. You should do so for a few reasons. You can:

- tailor the case specifically to your class and its personalities,
- better align your required curriculum and the objectives of the case,
- control all aspects of the case, and
- better understand the process of how a case is set up.

The most valuable of these would be the ability to tailor the case specifically to your class. For instance, if you have a class of more advanced learners, the research you include in the case might be at

DOI: 10.4324/9781003233428-7

a higher reading level. If, however, you gave the exact same case to a different class, the students may not be able to comprehend the research as is. You would have to find different, more accessible research for them to use.

The personalities of your class also play a factor. If you have a number of students who love to perform, you may want to set up your case to showcase these talents by having the product that shows mastery be a performance assessment. If your students are more reserved, the product might be something they produce, such as a brief or an exhibition, but not something they have to perform.

The level of experience of the class also is important to consider. If you are implementing your students' first case, you do not want to start them with a subtle and nuanced case because their lack of familiarity with the way cases run might cause them to overlook important aspects. Instead, you want to make the research and objectives of the case a little more obvious so that students can become more comfortable with the learning strategy. More than likely, students will not have used this method of teaching prior to your class, so you want to ease them into it. Depending on how the first case goes, you can scaffold the next case, making it more challenging because your students will be more used to the CBL process and can feel at ease digging a little deeper into the content.

Tailoring the case to fit your students also makes the learning more personalized because you can try to find cases and issues that might be more relevant to them. For instance, if a science class is looking at a case involving the dumping of hazardous materials, you might find research from a local spill so that students develop a solution to a case from their own community.

This chapter details a template for how to write your own case.

STEPS TO WRITING A CASE

Here are the basic steps to writing your own case study. You must develop:

1. a topic,
2. a title,
3. big picture questions for students to ponder,
4. an executive summary,
5. a description of what or who the case study is about (telling the story),
6. problems that were faced,
7. constraints of the case,
8. a review of the research that supports or refutes the case, and
9. an outline of the outcome of the actual case for discussion.

Even though all of these steps should be followed, they do not have to be followed in sequential order. For instance, you might not be able to develop a title to your case until you have researched it a little and have a better grasp of its subject matter. It might actually be the last thing you do, and that is alright. Or, you might happen upon an article and decide it would be a good topic for a case or find a collection of research before you even begin to write the case. The order is not important. Sometimes it is best to let a case organically grow itself. Whatever order that occurs in does not matter and would certainly be better than forcing it. For the sake of this chapter, we will go in order of the steps.

Choosing a Topic

When choosing a topic, there are a few routes you could take. Choose a topic that:

- aligns to your curriculum,
- is of high interest to students because of its timeliness or relevance,
- is potentially controversial and will provide plenty of content for students to explore,
- is a local issue so that students can actually put their solution into action, and/or
- will allow students to use the skills you want them to learn.

No matter which way you decide to go, there are a few things to consider if you want your case study to include enough material for students to develop into a meaningful solution. A high-quality case (Lynn, 1999):

- poses a problem that has no obvious right answer,
- identifies roles for people who must solve the problem and make decisions,
- requires the reader to use the information in the case to address the problem,
- requires the reader to think critically and analytically in order to evaluate the problem and potential solutions, and
- has enough information for a good analysis (pp. 117–118).

You do have to walk a balance beam when it comes to your case. Many times you are presenting something to students that actually happened, so you want to make sure to include facts and not embellish the story to the point that the true events get lost. You do not want students to get so wrapped up in the story that they lose sight of the problems the case presents. That is why it is a good idea to provide opportunities for discussion. A discussion:

- provides a summary if there has been a lot of information presented,
- engages your students with a hook or cliffhanger if you leave them with an essential question to think about as they move into the next part of the case,
- helps students orient themselves in the case, and
- keeps students focused.

The example that will be used throughout this chapter to illustrate how to set up a case is the trial of Dred Scott and its impact on the start of the Civil War. This is an appropriate topic because it is a case that involves lots of analysis, is very debatable, and is one of the major reasons the Civil War broke out, so there will be plenty of high-quality discussion generated by it. To create an authentic learning environment, students will get the opportunity not only to read about the case, but also to participate in it by holding a mock trial, using issues and witnesses from the actual case.

Developing a Title

You might think that the title of the case has no bearing on its effectiveness as a learning tool, but there are instances in which it actually does. Keep in mind that the title is the first impression a student has when presented with a case. You want to have something that is going to grab students' attention and make them excited to take on the case. If you have a title that is general or off-putting, students might not be enthusiastic about working on the case.

Let us say you have a case about a town whose water supply is found to have contaminants. The case is about determining who caused the pollution and what can be done to clean the water supply. You could have a title such as "The Polluted River." This title is short, to the point, and accurate in its description, but incredibly boring. This is not a book you would pick up or a movie you would want to see. At the same time, you do not want to be overdramatic with a title such as "The River That Destroyed a Town." This title is certainly more attention-grabbing but may be a little over the top. Like most things in life, there needs to be a balance when it comes to the title of your case. Part of it needs to be informative, but part of it also has to get students excited about the prospects it offers. A happy medium might be "Healing the Wounded River." This lets students know they will be trying to solve the problem of a polluted or "wounded" river, but at the same time, the title is catchy enough that it creates empathy for the case.

As for the Dred Scott trial, you could go with a straightforward title such as "The Trial of Dred Scott." Again, keeping in the spirit of creating intrigue and excitement, a better title might be "The Trial That Split Our Nation."

Is a catchy name going to make or break your case? Probably not, but the title is going to be the introduction to the case. Don't you want students to be excited about what the case might hold?

Big Picture Questions to Ponder

Next come the essential questions. These act as the backbone to the case and usually delve into the big picture or overarching themes. These questions should be thought-provoking and open-ended as much as possible to allow room for students to form their own opinions. You can think of these big picture questions as the takeaways. When a student finishes the case, the answers to these questions should form the main ideas you would like him or her to understand. Because of this, many times these essential questions will overlap with the learning objectives you or the students have developed for the case. Because we are in a standards-based education environment, often you would want to have the standard(s) listed as an essential question. Take, for instance, this grades 9–10 language arts content standard from the Common Core State

Standards: "Determine the central ideas or information of a primary or secondary source; provide an accurate summary of how key events or ideas develop over the course of the text."

You might have a case in which you ask students to use both primary and secondary sources to develop their solution for the case. The question could be "Which is more effective, a primary or secondary source, in providing an unbiased viewpoint of the case?" This would be a good essential question to include to make sure students are focused on this skill while working on the case.

When creating your essential questions, you can do them yourself, or you could make them together as a class. Either way, you should have around three to five of them. If you have a single essential question, you are limiting your students in what they can learn. If you have more than half a dozen, then things are going to get overlooked or lost.

Here is an example of essential questions that can be used for the Dred Scott case:

- What were the major issues the Supreme Court was considering in the Dred Scott case?
- What role did the Dred Scott trial have in the starting of the Civil War?
- How does an American court case function?

Notice that the last essential question listed here does not pertain to just the Dred Scott trial but instead refers to an ancillary effect of holding a mock trial for this particular case. Students will need to follow many of the same procedures as the American court system. This ensures that students are not only leaving the case with a good understanding of what the Dred Scott trial meant to our nation and how it helped to lead to the Civil War, but also learning how the court system works.

The essential questions should involve the ideas and content that you want students to pay attention to the most. There will be other shiny things that will distract them from what you want them to be learning, and the essential questions act as a beacon to bring students back to the more important aspects of the case.

Executive Summary

The executive summary should provide a brief overview of the case so that students can get a general idea of what they will be studying. It is always better for students to have a basic understanding of the premise before the dive into deeper issues. An executive summary for our Dred Scott case would look like this:

> When Dred Scott, a slave of a former military man, asks to buy his freedom from the wife who inherited him, she refuses. This causes him to take legal action, asking to be freed based on the fact that, while traveling with his owner, he lived in free states and territories. Using a legal precedent (*Winny v. Whitesides*), Scott's lawyers claim that "once free, always free" and that Scott and his wife should be granted their freedom. Should Dred Scott be set free or remain a slave? This is a decision the entire nation is waiting to hear.

Just like the title, a well-written executive summary is not going to make a case great, but it is certainly a good first step toward engaging students.

What or Who Is Your Case Study About (Telling the Story)

When creating your case, it is very important to find the story. Find what is at the heart of the case. What is it that people should care about? What is memorable about the case? Here is a good example of the power of a story:

After her birth, Amelia's parents learned their daughter had severe hypertrophic cardiomyopathy, a disease that makes it harder for the heart to pump blood to other parts of her body.

Amelia's condition meant she needed a new heart, but in order to get to that point, she needed several blood transfusions. That meant she relied on the donations of others to provide blood. Without these donations, she would not have the blood she needed and would likely die.

After several blood transfusions, at 8 months old Amelia was able to leave the hospital with a new heart. A new heart would not have been possible without the kindness of blood donors. Would you be willing to give blood so that others like Amelia can live a long and prosperous life?

Amelia's story is presented in great contrast to the following:

Hypertrophic cardiomyopathy (HCM) refers to an abnormal growth of muscle fibers in the heart. Because the heart muscle is stiff, it makes it difficult for it to relax and for blood to fill the heart chambers. Although the heart beats normally, the limited filling prevents the heart from pumping enough blood.

HCM is most often diagnosed during infancy or adolescence. It affects up to 500,000 people in the United States, with children under age 12 accounting for 10% of all cases. It is considered to be one of the most common causes of death in young people under 35 years of age. Children with HCM are usually asymptomatic, and the overall annual mortality beyond the first year of life is 1%.

> One blood donation can potentially save three lives. Every two seconds, someone needs blood. Blood cannot be manufactured. It can only be supplied by people such as yourself. Why wouldn't you want to give blood?

Which one of these stories is more persuasive? More importantly, which one makes you care? Most likely, the first one would be the one to tug at the heartstrings a little more, which is interesting because the second one actually shows how HCM affects more people, half a million to be exact. The first story affects a single person, but you get to hear this person's individual story. It is not a nameless, faceless statistic; this is Amelia.

You want to find the story for your case. You want to find what will make students care about the subject. This can be especially challenging when learning about something that happened years ago, but the way to make students care about the past and see the significance of learning about it, is by using the stories. That is how history gets remembered. What is the better story? There have been many important events that have occurred in the world that have been overshadowed by lesser events that told a better story. Consider the story of Paul Revere. You know the story: Paul Revere rode at midnight, racing through the streets of colonial America, warning the townsfolk that the British were coming. Because of his courage, the people were able to be ready for the British soldiers.

The interesting thing is that Paul Revere was not very successful in his ride. There were actually three riders—Paul Revere, William Dawes, and Samuel Prescott. All three were detained by the British soldiers, but Dawes and Prescott escaped, with only Prescott finishing his ride. Revere actually gave the British commanders information about the colonists before he was released. And yet why do we not celebrate the success of Prescott rather than the mediocre ride of Revere? Because the story of Paul Revere was immortalized in the 1861 poem "Paul Revere's Ride" by Henry Wadsworth Longfellow. The poem begins:

Listen, my children, and you shall hear
Of the midnight ride of Paul Revere,
On the eighteenth of April, in Seventy-Five:
Hardly a man is now alive
Who remembers that famous day and year.

This poem made Revere famous because it told a story.

Dred Scott is a perfect example of what happens when you tell a story. The issue of slavery had been debated for a long time with people making arguments for both sides. However, Dred Scott gave the issue a specific face. No longer were thousands of White people telling thousands of Black people that they could not be free. This was an instance of the U.S. government telling a single person whether he could be free or not. Harriet Beecher Stowe did the same thing when she wrote *Uncle Tom's Cabin*. Her work told the story of slavery—not just the ethics of the practice. It showed what happened to an individual who was affected by slavery.

Here is the story of Dred Scott:

> Dred Scott was born into slavery around 1799. After being sold to a couple of different farmers, he ended up with John Emerson, who was a surgeon in the U.S. Army. As an officer, Emerson frequently moved, taking Scott with him to Illinois. He also took him to the territory of Wisconsin. There were times when Scott, unhappy with the way he was being treated, would escape. It would never be for that long, however, and he was always returned to Emerson.
>
> Dred eventually married a fellow slave named Harriet. And even though slave marriages were not considered legal, her ownership was transferred to Emerson. While Emerson moved around, the Scotts were rented out to other soldiers. Emerson eventually married a woman named Irene

CASE STUDIES AND CASE-BASED LEARNING

and sent for the Scotts to live in Louisiana with them. When John died a few years later, Irene inherited his estate, including the Scotts, and leased them out to other people—not a positive experience for most slaves. Irene and her brother did not treat the Scotts well. She occasionally beat him and imprisoned him for hours. Because of this treatment, Scott offered to buy his own freedom, paying $300 to do so. Irene refused.

Then, Scott learned of the legal precedent of "once free always free." Because he had lived in the free state of Illinois and spent time in the free territory of Wisconsin, he was legally free. Although he was unable to read or write, he was helped in filing a case to get his freedom.

Here was a man who had spent his entire life being a slave, working only to have his wages given to others, who simply wanted to be free, which was his legal right. Because it was not permitted, he had never been taught to read or write, and all of his family members suffered from slavery as well. His story is like that of many other slaves during this time, but at the same time it is his story.

You might not be able to lock on to someone as specific as Dred Scott in your own case. However, every case has a story behind it. The question is: Can you find a case compelling enough to pull students in?

Problems That Were Faced

The problems of the case have probably already been shared in either the essential question or the executive summary. Regardless, it is important to make sure that they are reiterated so that students keep them central to the case. This section is a good place to provide context for the problem. For example, say that you have students in math class who have been given the case of rebuilding the San Francisco Giants baseball team for the 2016 baseball season (in an alternate universe in which the team might win the World Series). The case will require students to greatly consider the team's finances. The problems students would need to consider include:

- putting together a team that can win the World Series,
- competing with the Los Angeles Dodgers who tend to spend more money than the Giants, and
- creating a reasonable budget that is not going to hamper the team for years to come.

As students analyze and research the problems, they will obtain the context they need in order to be successful with their solution. For the Dred Scott case, the problems might include:

- whether Dred Scott has a legal right to his freedom,
- the fact that slaves did not have the same rights as U.S. citizens, and
- the effect the outcome of this court case could have on the country as a whole.

Throughout the case, students need to be aware that 150 years ago, it was legal to own another human being and require that person to work. Slaves also were not considered citizens and possessed no legal rights, not even being allowed to be legally married. That is the before-the-case context. The after-the-case context is the effect that the Dred Scott case had on the Civil War. When the Supreme Court rendered its verdict in the Dred Scott case in 1857, the court essentially ruled that Black people have no rights and made slavery legal anywhere in the United States, not just the South. This angered the Northern abolitionists and escalated the tension between the two sides, eventually leading to violence and the start of the Civil War.

Constraints of the Case

The constraints of a case include the limiting factors that have to be considered by the teacher as well as those working on the case. For instance, if your case is looking at how humans put a man into orbit around the planet, a constraint would be what technology was available at that time; a computer that now fits in our pockets in the form of our cell phones would have occupied a very large room or might not have been available at all. Or if your case involves the current treatment of women in Saudi Arabia, you cannot simply suggest that they abandon their culture and history overnight. You would have to work within the current culture to figure out a solution.

Constraints can include issues such as:

- budget,
- time,
- history,
- culture, or
- science/technology.

Constraints can be helpful. They can make sure that students are being realistic and creative with their solutions.

In the case of Dred Scott, students might be required to:

- utilize the American court system and procedures,
- abide by and follow the procedures of a real-life court, and
- consider the culture and economy of the time.

While working on the case, the students must take all of these factors into consideration to arrive at a feasible solution. This is not to say that students cannot be innovative and creative, thinking outside of the box with their solution. There are just certain boxes they cannot go outside of.

Research That Supports or Refutes the Case

The major difference between case-based learning and problem-based learning is that in PBL students are tasked with finding much of the information themselves. If they are trying to solve the problem of illegal immigration, they would seek reliable sources that would present information for both sides of the argument. They would be responsible for finding their sources. Through case-based learning, the teacher often provides the main document the students will be reading to learn the information they need to construct their solution. The teacher can choose documents that are commensurate to students' reading levels. A high school class might be looking at research written at the university level, while a fourth-grade class may have documents that are written with kids as their primary audience in mind.

Teachers provide students with these main documents in order to control the information. This is because there is a lot of information out there. This is not to say that you should not teach students how to determine the reliability of a document for themselves. Technology literacy is a valuable life skill for students to understand, and, considering that a majority of our news and research will come from online, it is something students should definitely know. By supplying the research yourself, you can rest easy, knowing that students are getting the information needed for the case from a reliable source. It also helps to provide sources that consider both sides, as there will be cases in which there are two sides to consider.

You might provide only a single document, which would act as your sole guide for students and where a majority of their information would come from that shapes their case. You might provide two documents, each arguing a side of the case so that students are seeing multiple perspectives and takes on the case. You could offer multiple documents, a mix of both primary and secondary documents that give the students a well-rounded explanation of the case.

In addition to the documents you provide, students are always able and encouraged to find their own supporting documents when necessary, especially if they need to research lots of possible solutions to the problem.

In the Dred Scott example, providing an unbiased but detailed overview of the case is going to be important because you want to make sure the trial is as fair as possible, sticking to facts and using characters that really were present. There are both primary and secondary documents that can be used. A primary document would be like the one found at https://cdn.loc.gov/service/rbc/rbaapc/09100/09100.pdf, which is a fair examination of the case by a newspaper in 1858 right after the trial. To see an example of a secondary document that provides a pretty comprehensive overview of the case, you can go to https://www.pbs.org/wgbh/aia/part4/4h2933t.html, which nicely lays out the issues involved that students will have to think about in their roles.

Outcome of the Actual Case for Discussion

Because there will be times that your case is based on something from the past that has a known outcome, there is no mystery as to the solution that actually occurred. This, of course, does not mean that your students have to come up with the same solution. In fact, many times they will want to avoid the actual solution because it either did not work or there was a better option that was not used. However, it is important for students to analyze the actual outcome so that they can learn from it and any possible mistakes or oversights that were made. This could be part of their actual case, or it could be in the form of a reflection after the fact in which students analyze and compare the different solutions and how effective they were.

For the trial of Dred Scott, the teacher can use the actual written opinions of judges who voted in favor and opposed, are available from the Library of Congress: https://cdn.loc.gov/service/ll/llst/020/020.pdf. These primary documents provide the context of the court decision from the judges' perspectives.

MAKING A CASE

Creating your own case can be time-consuming and involved, but using this structure can help to streamline the process and provide you with guidance as to how a case should be set up. With the steps outlined in this chapter, you should be able to create compelling cases that will help your students gain an enduring understanding of myriad topics. Remember, you might be able to find cases that already exist, but by writing your own, you personalize the case to your students, your class curriculum, and yourself.

Some factors to consider while constructing your case, as suggested by EduTech Wiki (2018), include:

- What is the case about?
- What are some of the potential learning issues?
- Can I differentiate the case?
- How difficult or obscure are the issues in the case?
- Will there be issues my students will care about?
- Is the case open-ended enough for students to go beyond fact finding?
- What do I see as possible areas for investigation?
- What product might I ask students to produce?

- Is the case too short or too long for the time I have available?
- What sorts of learning resources might be needed for this case? Are they accessible?
- If I use this case, what lectures/labs/discussions might I want to change, add or eliminate? (sec. 6.3)

By pondering these factors you will begin to come up with the various parts of your case, such as the big questions, constraints, and the story behind the case.

CHAPTER 5

PURPOSEFULLY TEACHING COLLABORATION

While working on a case, students are likely going to have to work in groups to develop a solution. This requires the skill of collaboration, which is one of the seven survival skills and one of the tenets of inquiry-based learning (Wagner, 2008). Collaboration is not a skill that comes naturally, however. Working well with others is a learned skill. Depending on the age of your students and their backgrounds, they may have already learned how to work well with others. At the same time, they might have picked up a lot of bad habits while engaging in group work in the past. It is important to be purposeful about teaching the skill of collaboration. In fact, teaching collaboration would probably greatly benefit your class if you spent the first couple of weeks of school or the semester to develop this particular skill. The rest of your year would go so much smoother with this training, especially if you plan on using a lot of case-based and inquiry-based learning in which students will be required to work in groups.

DOI: 10.4324/9781003233428-8

This chapter lays out what 2 weeks of collaboration training might look like. If you do not feel it is necessary to spend an entire 2 weeks on collaboration, you can pick and conduct the lessons that you think would be most valuable for your students:

- Day 1: Challenge/Discussion
- Day 2: Setting Norms
- Day 3: Skills Inventory
- Day 4: Determining Roles
- Day 5: Group Dynamics
- Day 6: Coping Mechanisms
- Days 7–9: Professional Amateurs Case
- Day 10: Anchoring Session/Reflection

Day 1: Challenge/Discussion

The first day of school might be the best time to explore how well students collaborate with one another (although these activities can be performed at other times). You have a classroom full of students—some of whom know each other and some of whom do not. What would be a better time to see how good they are at working together in groups?

1. Divide students into random groups, either using the alphabet, assigning them numbers, or using whose birthdays are closest.
2. Assign each group a task that is nearly impossible to accomplish. A really simple one that does not require many materials is the square puzzle. You can use the template in Figure 4. Here are the constraints of the puzzle:
   - Each group has 5 minutes to try to put the pieces into the shape of a square.
   - Groups must use all seven pieces.
   - None of the pieces should overlap.
   - Groups must create a square (all sides should be equal in length).

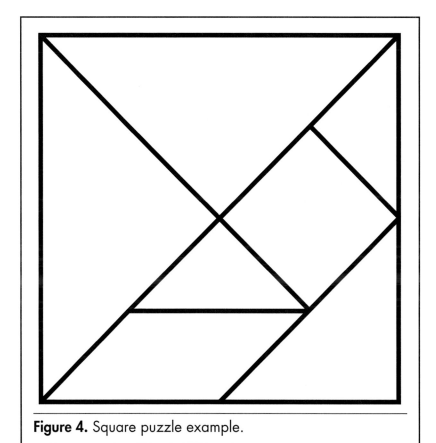

Figure 4. Square puzzle example.

3. Set a timer for 5 minutes and walk around the room and make observations. You might observe:
   - one person doing all of the work,
   - a group divided into factions and each working on its own approach,
   - a group arguing over the solution,
   - a group giving up,
   - a group working very well together but not getting anywhere, or
   - lots and lots of chaos.

4. If, by some chance, one group solves the square, let the clock keep running until the 5 minutes are up.

5. When the time is up, stop the groups. Check whether anyone completed the square or not. Then, have students privately rate themselves on how well they think their group worked together. Provide students with a set of reflection questions to think about. Those questions might include:
    ◆ What went right in your group?
    ◆ What went wrong in your group?
    ◆ What specific actions led to you feeling as though the group was successful?
    ◆ What specific actions led to you feeling as though the group did not work well?
    ◆ What could have been done to improve the way the group worked?
    ◆ Just because your group did not complete the task, does that make it a failure?
    ◆ Do you see much value in working in groups to complete a task?
    ◆ If you were putting groups together, how would you do so?
    ◆ Would you rather work in a group effectively with someone you do not like or work with someone you do like who does not produce quality work?
    ◆ Do you see the long-term value in learning how to work well in a group?

6. After giving students some time to think about these questions individually, have them use the philosophical chairs protocol to get them out of their seats and engaged. To do so, rephrase the discussion questions as agree or disagree statements:
    ◆ I feel more went right in my group than went wrong.
    ◆ My group tried many different strategies in order to find the one that would work best.

- There were specific actions by people in my group that made it difficult to work as a team.
- There are slight changes that could be made in order to improve the way the group worked.
- I feel like we failed because we were unable to complete the task.
- I think that working in a group, if done well, can produce better work than if I had worked on it by myself.
- Often times I feel as though one or two people do all of the work and everyone else is just along for the ride.
- I like working in groups but only if the right people are put in my group.
- I prefer to pick my friends to be in my group.
- I despise working in groups.

7. Designate one side of the room for those who agree with the statement and the opposite side of the room for those who disagree. Read aloud the statements one at a time, and have students move to whichever side of the room represents their feelings. This will organically create two opposing groups. Have each side take turns defending its position. You should act as a bystander in this back and forth, although you will want to cite examples of your observations as you moved around and watched the groups work, when appropriate. Once the debate begins to wane, read the next statement.

8. After getting through all of the statements, if there is class time left, summarize the takeaways from the discussion, writing down four or five of them. Some of these takeaways might be:
   - There are certainly advantages to working in groups.
   - Group work is fine when everyone pulls his or her weight.
   - The way groups are chosen can sometimes make no sense.

♦ There should be a way to make everyone accountable in the group.
♦ When groups are bad, it can be a disaster.

Day 2: Setting Norms

Day 1 was designed to have students think about what they like or dislike about working in groups. Day 2 is about establishing what they need in order to be successful in group work. This involves establishing norms. Norms are different than rules. Rules are typically created by the authority figure and decreed. The rules are followed because students are worried about getting in trouble. Rules are all about compliance and are usually solely enforced by the authority figure in the classroom. Norms are expectations that are agreed upon by everyone. Norms are not created by a single person, but rather by all of those who are expected to live up to them. As a result, they are not necessarily enforced by the authority figure. Anyone in the class can enforce a norm, and rather than receiving a punishment, should someone go against a norm, he or she is reminded of the norm and to be responsible for his or her own actions. Norms are way more effective than rules because students had a role in creating them, meaning they are going to remember them better and care more about them.

Creating norms for working in groups can go a long way in having much smoother group dynamics. Norms are unique to each class, meaning if you have five different classes, you might have five different sets of norms. The important thing about norms is making sure that the students are part of the process of creating them:

1. Give everyone in the class access to a pad of sticky notes. Ask students to consider the following question: What do you need in order to be successful in a group?
2. Ask students to phrase their answers in a positive manner (i.e., rather than writing what people should not do, students should consider what people should do). Ask for students to

write down as many norms as they like. Recommend that they have at least four to five, and suggest to them that, if they have fewer than that, then they are effectively taking away their own voice in the shaping of the classroom norms. They are welcome to have more as well. Make sure to allow for plenty of time for students to think and answer. If some students finish quickly, do not feel compelled to move on. Give everyone time to develop their sticky notes.

3. Once everyone has finished, have students work in groups to create affinity diagrams. Divide students into small groups of about five. Have them bring their sticky notes to a clear space, whether it be a white board, a bare wall, or butcher paper. One student begins by placing his or her sticky notes into distinctive groups. Others will then read the sticky notes already posted and see if they have any that match the groups. If a sticky note matches, the other students should lay their sticky note with the others. Matches may not be perfect but should include the same general idea. For example, one student might have phrased a norm as, "Work without having to be told to." Another student may have written, "Show initiative." The two are close enough in spirit to be a match, meaning they should be placed together.

4. As the entire class begins to place their sticky notes, the tenets of successful collaboration that are most important to the class will begin to emerge naturally, resulting in a class-wide affinity diagram.

5. As the teacher, manage who is coming up to the diagram as well as organize the sticky notes, helping students to match similar statements and grouping those that belong together. Through this process, you will probably have four to seven much larger collections of sticky notes. These are what form the norms for the class. You might have to wordsmith occasionally or reframe a student's written statement to a positive one, but the main ideas the students developed are still present. Some examples of norms that groups tend to come up with include:

- Everyone does his or her role/pulls his or her weight.
- Listen to everyone's ideas.
- Make contributions positive.
- Allow time/space for processing (the first answer is not always the best one).
- Move forward if your idea is not chosen.
- If you finish your work, find other ways to help the group rather than being done.
- Produce quality work.
- Be respectful.
- Be willing to refocus when asked by others.

6. Try to have no more than four to seven norms for a class; otherwise they become white noise, and none of them are really followed. You will also want to make sure that you allow all voices to be heard in this process. That means the sticky notes that did not find a large following should be read and addressed. Many times these are issues specific to a particular student, or they can be altered a little to fit under some of the larger statements. You do not want to ignore ideas students shared. You want to make sure you are modeling what you hope to see from students when they are working together.

7. Develop norms with all of your classes, starting over each time rather than using the previous class's responses with another group of students. Each class will arrive at the similar conclusions, but the process of students arriving there on their terms is important in order for them to feel a part of the decision making.

8. Once the norms are formed, type them and distribute copies, or display them somewhere in the classroom. It is important to refer to the norms as much as possible, especially at the beginning. When students become familiar with the norms, students will be able to help you to enforce them. In an ideal classroom, you will not have act as enforcer. The

students will remind themselves of the norms and monitor progress independently.

Day 3: Skills Inventory

For Day 3, students will participate in a self-assessment, determining what skills they bring to group work. This can be tricky because, although some students might be very aware of their skillset, there are others who may not have an understanding of what they are actually good at.

1. Provide students with a list of skills that collaboration might require, such as the self-assessment in Figure 5. You might shorten or lengthen this list depending upon the age and abilities of your students.

2. Review each of the skills with the class and either provide an illustration for what that skill might look like in a group setting or ask students for examples of what they think it might look like. You will want to caution students that the goal is not to check as many boxes as possible. The goal is to get a clear indication of what skills students possess and can use.

3. Students might even want to audit the list. After a student has completed a list, he or she should share with another student or two, preferably ones that are familiar with working with him or her, to determine whether the student's list is accurate or not. The student might not have included skills that his or her colleagues believe he or she is skilled at, or the student might include skills that, in reality, are not his or her strongest. Everyone wants to believe they are a good leader, but the reality is that not that many people are. Some may equate a skill with leadership, while others might just view it as bossiness. Give your students time and space to have these conversations to make sure the skills inventory paints a clear picture.

- ❏ Adaptability—deals with change well, does not panic
- ❏ Advanced computer skills—good with technology, including software and programs
- ❏ Artistic—artistically creative and able to work with many media
- ❏ Caring—able to empathize with others and be sensitive to their feelings
- ❏ Creative thinking—able to come up with new ideas, thinks of unique solutions
- ❏ Critical thinking—looks at a problem from many angles and considers all choices
- ❏ Decision making—able to be assertive when making decisions
- ❏ Financial—keeps accurate records and can manage a budget
- ❏ Interviewing—able to ask good questions of people that get helpful information
- ❏ Leadership—motivates others to act, helps to keep group moving forward
- ❏ Logical thinking—can draw reasonable conclusions from facts and ideas
- ❏ Mediation—able to resolve conflict in an open and positive manner
- ❏ Negotiating—good at discussing and bargaining with others to make compromises
- ❏ Oral communication—presents ideas and opinions in a clear and confident manner
- ❏ Organization—able to prioritize tasks in order to meet deadlines
- ❏ Performing—able to make presentations that entertain and inform
- ❏ Problem solving—able to look at various options and develop a viable solution
- ❏ Public speaking—can make formal presentations to a professional audience
- ❏ Research—knows how to find and collect information that is relevant
- ❏ Teaching—able to create an effective learning environment
- ❏ Technological—understands technical systems and can operate them effectively
- ❏ Writing—able to organize and clearly communicate key ideas in written form

Figure 5. Example skills inventory.

Day 4: Determining Roles

Many people think of group work and imagine that everyone should be doing the exact same type and amount of work. But is this fair? If each student has a specific skill set, should you not take advantage of that? Or if you have someone who is not particularly good at a skill, do you want that person taking part and causing the quality of the product to suffer? Would you not want the person who is best at something to be responsible for that skill should it be needed by the group?

One of the biggest issues with group work is the grade equity issue. Typically, the entire group gets a single grade for its work. If Student 1 feels as though she did 50% of the work, and Student 2 did around 10%, it does not seem fair if the group receives an A. Student 1 did most of the work. Why should Student 2 get the same grade as her? Conversely, if that group instead gets a C because Student 2 did not perform adequately, is that fair to Student 1? How do you allow students to work in groups and still have fair grading practices?

There are a couple of approaches to take with this. The first one involves the use of peer and self-evaluations to shape the overall grade. Throughout a case, you can have students evaluate each other's work every few days. In each of these check-ins, students can evaluate each member of the group and themselves with a letter grade and provide written justification for the assigned grade. Teachers may need to coach students on what this looks like. If a student gives a groupmate a B and justifies that with the comment, "good work," what does that look like? Through their writing, you need to have students show, not just tell. Students should consider detailed and constructive comments.

Following these evaluations throughout the case, a group's final grade should indicate each group member's contributions. If the group receives a B as an overall grade, but a student's self- and peer evaluations average out to an A, then that student's grade should be a B+ or even an A-. If, on the other hand, a member of that same group receives a D average on the self- and peer evaluations, then his or her grade should drop to a C or C-. These self- and peer evaluations act as a calibration of the group grade, properly rewarding students who do good work and giving those students who did not contribute as much a more accurate reflection of their work.

There are, of course, variables to consider when it comes to this method. You are asking 30 children to evaluate each another. Each student brings his or her own biases to the table, meaning valid and reliable scores might be difficult to achieve. Student 1 might give Student 2 an A because Student 1 is a nice person, but Student 3 might give Student 2 a D because Student 3 does not like Student 2. Even without these extremes, what one student might see as A work another might characterize as B work. There is also the issue of collusion, where groupmates agree to give each other high marks even though they did not work well, or two friends decide to help each other out. Typically, groups are big enough that the truth comes out in the other evaluations as well as teacher observations. Regardless, students must be trained to know what good work looks like. While students adjust to conducting self- and peer evaluations, try anchoring grades at first until everyone understands the expectations.

The second method of having a more fair group grade is making students responsible for a specific role that they are then accountable for. Here are examples of general roles students could assume:

- **Coordinator:** Keeps the group on-task and makes sure everyone gets a say.
- **Scribe:** Writes down the group's findings and discussions.
- **Spokesperson:** Orally communicates updates and group's findings to the teacher or class when necessary.
- **Manager:** Makes sure the group is using its time well and reminds the group of impending deadlines.
- **Quality control:** Is responsible for making sure the end product is of high quality and done to the specifications of the group.

If the group presents its product and there is a problem with some of the research, then the scribe would be the one responsible and his grade might be lower than that of the other group members. Or if the product is very professional-looking, the quality control person might get a higher grade because she was accountable for that aspect and its success or failure.

Depending on the case, roles might be a little more specific, such as the following:

- **Head of research:** Oversees the research the group does and makes sure it is acting as evidence toward the group's case.
- **Presenter:** Is in charge of presenting the findings to the authentic audience.
- **Facilitator:** Keeps the group on task and aware of coming deadlines.
- **Liaison:** Is in charge of communication between the teacher and the group.
- **Oversight:** Is in charge of making sure the group is following criteria for the assessment of the case as laid out in the syllabus, rubric, or briefing.

During a scenario in which the case is an actual court case, the roles would be assigned depending on the parts you need fulfilled. There could be lawyers, judges, witnesses, jury members, etc. Students would then be responsible for their role, and you would grade them individually even though they acted as part of a larger group.

You could start with a list of possible roles that members could take on and let each group decide for itself which parts need to be filled. Using the skills inventory, students might be assigned roles depending on what they are good at. Keep in mind that just because someone is responsible for an aspect does not mean he or she is the only one who works on it. It simply means that he or she is responsible for the quality of the work that the group produces for that role. There are all sorts of various strategies for choosing students' roles, but the important thing is that each student has something he or she can individually be held accountable for, so that the grade reflects each student's work rather than the group's.

Here is an activity you can do on this day. Have students choose one skill from their inventory sheet that they feel they are best at. Then form groups of five, doing your best not to have any repeats of the same skill in a group. Then give the groups the following task:

> You have been exiled to a deserted island for a year. You may choose five essential items the group will use to survive. In addition, you may bring one of each of the following for the group:
> - a book to read,
> - a piece of music to listen to,
> - a board game to play,
> - a comfort item, or
> - a box of cookies (you must choose the brand).
>
> What would you take and why?

Give groups an allotted amount of time to make their decisions. Students must explain why the items were chosen and how they will help them to survive. During this time, students can use any resources at their disposal. When the time is up, each group must present its choices to the class.

Day 5: Group Dynamics

This day will be spent as a reflection on the activity from the day before. Specifically, students will look at how well their group worked together and what could be done to improve the dynamics between group members.

You can choose to do this reflection in a number of ways. You could have students journal their thoughts privately before sharing them with others. You could have each group run its own discussion. You could have two groups get together and interview each other. You could lead a whole-class discussion. Whichever method you choose, use these guiding questions to generate discussion:

- Were you pleased with the way things turned out?
- Did your group have any difficulties making decisions together?
- What could the group have done a better job of?
- Did everyone in the group feel listened to?
- What do you feel the group did really well together?
- Did people take the roles they were assigned seriously?
- Was having the roles helpful to the group?
- How do you think these roles would work on a long-term project?
- How did your group settle differences of opinion? Do you think this was the best way to handle this?
- If there was anything you could have changed about your group, what would it be?
- Do you think you were more successful as a group making these decisions than you would have been on your own?

As you go over these questions with students, take note of any problems or issues that are mentioned by students. You will be addressing these and many more the following day.

Day 6: Coping Mechanisms

This is a day during which students are going to become problem solvers. They will develop strategies to help them to overcome any difficulties while working in groups. With your help they will develop coping mechanisms that they will use throughout the year whenever they are collaborating with other students.

The most common problems people have when working in a group are:

- figuring out how to get started,
- members not contributing,
- people not following the norms,
- ideas not becoming fully formed,
- disagreements between team members,
- getting off task,
- bad communication or lack of listening,
- one or two people dominating the group,
- members not doing their roles or trying to do others' roles, and
- not meeting the deadline or objectives of the lesson provided.

You could teach coping mechanisms for each of these in a few ways. First, you might have a class discussion about each of them, generating answers from the students and ways they have coped with these issues in the past. Secondly, you could create a cheat sheet that you could talk about as a class, or you can have students discuss in their groups. This cheat sheet can be pulled out and used throughout the year. Some cheat sheet examples for each issue might include:

- Figuring out how to get started:
  - Take time for all members to introduce themselves and their specific strengths.
  - Decide on jobs or roles for each member.
  - Develop an agenda and a timeline.

- Members not contributing:
  - Establish why the group believes a member is not contributing.
  - Make sure that the person who is being accused of not contributing gets his or her say.

- ◆ Ensure that each member gets his or her turn to contribute; this may mean going around the circle.

- People not following the norms:
  - ◆ Have a copy of the norms to reference when it appears someone is not following them.
  - ◆ Remind the groupmate of the norm rather than pointing out his or her behavior.
  - ◆ Revisit and revise the norms if need be.

- Ideas not becoming fully formed:
  - ◆ Do more brainstorming where you focus on long-term questions, such as "What if . . .?" and "What else . . .?"
  - ◆ Ask each member individually to jot down or share ideas.
  - ◆ As more ideas are created, organize further research individually and then meet up as a team later to reassess.

- Disagreements between team members:
  - ◆ Show that you have heard other members' ideas and when disagreeing do so politely and respectfully.
  - ◆ Make sure everyone in the group knows what it means to compromise.
  - ◆ Sometimes it is good to just take a break and reconvene later.

- Getting off task:
  - ◆ Create a calendar and refer to it often.
  - ◆ Make sure you have a manager or leader amongst your group roles who will make sure no one is getting off task; if you do not have one, make someone in charge of this role.
  - ◆ Call for a group meeting when it appears someone is getting off task and have group members report on their current progress.

- Bad communication or lack of listening:
    - Identify specific triggers that seem to affect communication.
    - If two people are having issues, have a third group member act as an impartial mediator.
    - Have a more formal meeting with the group where each person reports on his or her progress.

- One or two people dominating the group:
    - Create time limits on individual contributions.
    - Make a protocol where each member has a chance to speak without interruption.
    - Look again at the roles and which people are supposed to be doing what tasks.

- Members not doing their roles or trying to do others' roles:
    - Remind each other of the roles that the group agreed to.
    - If unclear, establish on a piece of paper what the group believes each role should encompass.
    - Have meetings as a group to check on the status of each person's role.

- Not meeting the deadline or objectives of the lesson provided:
    - Either look at the calendar or at the rubric to make sure tasks will be completed on time and with high quality.
    - Ask each member to present a progress report on what he or she has completed lately.
    - If one person is struggling, offer to assist to complete tasks if necessary (this does not mean taking over the role).

A third option would be to give each group a couple of the problems. Assign groups to create a skit or scenario where they figure out ways to solve the issue. Have groups perform these skits to the class and discuss further.

Whichever strategy you decide to use, students should leave this day with a clear understanding of the sorts of conflicts they might run into while collaborating and, more importantly, what strategies they can use when issues arise in their groups.

Days 7–9: Professional Amateurs Case

Now you are going to practice what you preach. The next 3 days will be spent conducting a mini-case by:

- reading over the case and assigning roles,
- working on a solution, and
- presenting a solution.

Have students form new groups. Tell students to try to match up skills again, only this time they cannot have anyone in the group that was a collaborator before. The following is an example case that students could work on. You might have teams of five to six students in each group, pairing up groups against one another. One group will argue for the paying of college athletes, with the other arguing against.

Choosing a topic: Should college athletes be paid?

Developing a title: The Big Business of Free Athletes

Big picture questions to ponder:

- Should college athletes be paid for playing sports and bringing in money for their schools?
- Is the promise of a scholarship worth all of the effort a college athlete commits to?
- Should the NCAA have the right to license and profit from student athletes?
- Would more college athletes stay in school longer if they were paid?

Executive summary: Currently, athletes who play college sports do not get paid a salary for doing so. They do get compensated with scholarships to attend college either for free or partially paid. Yet the NCAA makes an average of $1 billion a year through these sporting events, television revenues, and selling the likeness of these athletes to various companies.

What or who is your case study about (telling the story): Consider the case of *O'Bannon v. NCAA* (2014). Ed O'Bannon was a college athlete who played basketball for UCLA. The NCAA would license out players' names and likenesses to videogame companies. O'Bannon argued that upon graduation, athletes should be financially compensated for the NCAA's commercial use of their image.

Problems that were faced: There was a case in 1984: *NCAA v. Board of Regents of the University of Oklahoma*. In that case the court ruled that the NCAA could preserve its amateurism and not pay its athletes.

Constraints of the case: There is the Sherman Antitrust Act, which affects college sports.

Research that supports or refutes the case: Have students watch a video produced by Business Insider concerning the pros and cons of paying college athletes: https://www.businessinsider.com/ncaa-college-athletes-march-madness-basketball-football-sports-not-paid-2019-3. Students can also read over the actual case at https://caselaw.findlaw.com/us-9th-circuit/1714344.html. High school students might also want to look at this review by the Western State University: https://lawscl.org/cgi/viewcontent.cgi?refer er=&httpsredir=1&article=1005&context=wslawreview.

Outcome of the actual case for discussion: The initial trial was overseen by the district judge, who ruled that schools should be allowed to offer full cost-of-attendance scholarships to athletes, as well as covering cost-of-living expenses that were not currently part of NCAA scholarships. It was also ruled that colleges be permitted to place as much as $5,000 into a trust for each athlete per year of eligibility. The case was appealed to the Supreme Court, which decided not to take the case.

While students practice going through a case, you can practice going around toward the end of class and conducting a status conference with all of the groups. On the second day, you can consider conducting a process conference with each group. On the presentation day, you can spend the first half of the class running design conferences to make sure each group's product is where it should be. What these conferences look like will be covered more in the next chapter.

Day 10: Reflection

Have students conduct a self- and peer assessment of their group members from days 7–9. Have students rate themselves and each groupmate on five aspects (see Figure 6 for an example). This means that if there are six members in the group, each person will fill out six of these forms. Students will assign a 0 through 10, 0 being the low end of the scale and 10 being the high. In addition, each student needs to explain in a sentence or two what evidence he or she has to justify this score.

Then the groups will take part in the final word protocol. The way this works is the group sits in a circle. One member's name is read, and he or she must remain quiet as the group goes around the circle, stating what score was given and the evidence to back it up. When the group gets back around to the original person, he or she can share his or her self-evaluated score as well as the evidence to rationalize it.

Once everyone has been rated, ask students to average their scores. Then, have them self-reflect on the following quietly either in a journal or on the computer. Their responses will be for their eyes only:
- Were the score your groupmates gave you and the one you gave yourself pretty close to one another?
- If the scores were not close, why do you think that is?

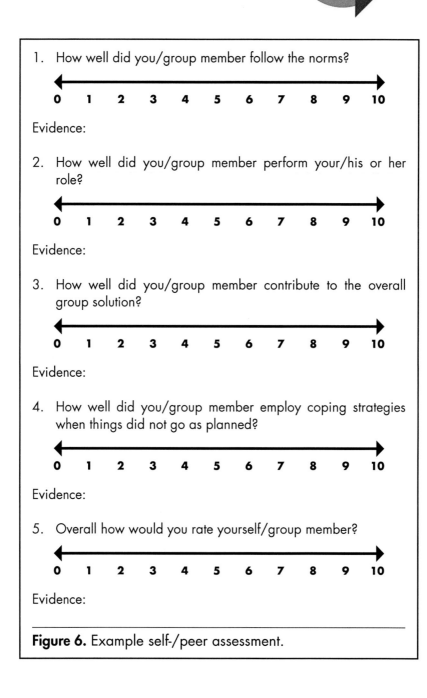

1. How well did you/group member follow the norms?

    0   1   2   3   4   5   6   7   8   9   10

Evidence:

2. How well did you/group member perform your/his or her role?

    0   1   2   3   4   5   6   7   8   9   10

Evidence:

3. How well did you/group member contribute to the overall group solution?

    0   1   2   3   4   5   6   7   8   9   10

Evidence:

4. How well did you/group member employ coping strategies when things did not go as planned?

    0   1   2   3   4   5   6   7   8   9   10

Evidence:

5. Overall how would you rate yourself/group member?

    0   1   2   3   4   5   6   7   8   9   10

Evidence:

Figure 6. Example self-/peer assessment.

- What could you have specifically done to have been a better contributor to the group?
- How well do you think your group worked together?
- If you could change one thing about one of your groupmates to have made the group run better, what would it have been?
- How do you think your group experience is going to go this school year? Is it something you are looking forward to or dreading?

MAKING A CASE

In order for case-based learning to work effectively, students must be able to work in groups successfully and collaborate. This is why it is imperative that you take some time to make sure students are trained properly how to do so.

You do not have to do all of the activities in this chapter, but the ones that are most important are setting norms, having students complete a skills inventory, and talking about coping mechanisms they can use to help solve problems. If you do these three at least, you will give your class a much better chance of finding success when working in groups.

CHAPTER 6

MANAGING THE CASE-BASED LEARNING CLASSROOM

As you have probably figured out by now, a majority of the work in case-based learning for the teacher is on the front end. You are either finding the case or creating it yourself. This takes time and effort and should be the hardest you work during the case-based learning process. Once the case is introduced and the students have begun to sink their teeth into it, the role of the teacher becomes quite different than in a typical, traditional classroom.

There have generally been two schools of thought as to the level of involvement of the teacher in the classroom. First is the more traditionally known sage on the stage. This involves the teacher standing in front of the classroom and disseminating information and knowledge. This can come in the form of a lecture, the demonstration of a math concept by doing problems on the board, or a discussion about a thought-provoking book in language arts class. The general tenet of the sage on the stage is that the teacher is the

 DOI: 10.4324/9781003233428-9

primary driver. He or she decides which vehicle to use. Whether it be a vehicle built for speed, for size, or for efficiency, he or she is hitting the accelerator and brakes to regulate the speed, and he or she is steering which direction the class is going to go and where students will end up.

This method can be exhausting to manage. Because you are the sage, you are front and center all of the time and have to maintain the control of the class. This requires your constant attention, and if you take your eyes off the road for even a moment, you might end up in a ditch. There are masterful sages on the stage who enthrall students with their storytelling abilities or their passion for the subject matter. Listening to a teacher who spends a week from every summer vacation visiting the battle sites for the Civil War talk about this very subject matter can be very educational and inspirational. A teacher who genuinely loves the book *The Great Gatsby* is going to be able to pass this love off to her students as she leads them through a discussion of the disparity between the classes in the book. A math teacher who takes really complicated mathematical processes and is able to explain them simply breaking them down step by step, and making them understandable, is going to be very effective when those students attempt a problem very similar to what was demonstrated.

There is a time and place for this type of teaching. There will even be moments during a case when you will take the sage approach, but most times, you will be taking on the second level of involvement, known as the guide on the side. Just as the name implies, in this method, the teacher is no longer front and center. Instead, the teacher is moving into the background, allowing students the space to explore topics on their own and make decisions for themselves. Students are responsible for what they learn, and just like a guide would do, the teacher points out some of the interesting scenery along the way, answers questions that might be asked, and occasionally stops the group to relay some information.

This type of teaching can be somewhat uncomfortable for some teachers, especially if they were taught in a very traditional setting.

The prospect of giving your students control over their learning can be a terrifying. So many questions pop into your head, such as "What if my students steer this project in the wrong direction?", "How will I ensure that the content standards on the year-end test will be mastered?", and "When are we going to fit all of this in to the semester?"

The main benefit to the guide approach is that, much like the saying, you are teaching your students to fish, or in this case, learn. Once they have figured out how to learn for themselves, anything is possible. Students no longer need someone to lead them in their learning. They can take full ownership of this great responsibility, taking some of that burden off of the teacher.

MEDDLER IN THE MIDDLE

The guide approach is one that is used in most forms of inquiry-based learning. In project-based learning, students are given the task of working in groups to produce a product that will show what they have learned. The teacher takes a backseat to the students, who are making many of the decisions, such as what form a product will take, who will be responsible for what, and how to go about creating the product. Problem-based learning runs along those same lines, with the students being given or finding their own problem and then developing a solution that will solve the problem. In both of these teaching strategies, the best thing the teacher can do is simply get out of the way. Provide students with the resources they need, give them some occasional advice when they ask for it, and be prepared to step in as only a last resort if things are not going well.

Case-based learning requires the teacher to walk the tight-rope between being sage on the stage and a guide on the side. The main role of the teacher in case-based learning is to ask thought-provoking questions of the students that are designed to challenge their thinking. The teacher becomes the meddler in the middle, stirring up things when they seem to be going smooth. According to McWilliam (2008),

> Meddling is a repositioning of teacher and student as co-directors and co-editors of their social world. As a learning partnership, meddling has powerful implications for what "content" is considered worthy of engagement, how the value of the learning product is to be assessed, and who the rightful assessor is to be. (p. 88)

Disruption is where the greatest learning takes place. Students need to be made a little uncomfortable in order to learn, and it is the role of the teacher in the case-based learning classroom to provide this environment. Teachers can do this by asking probing questions that make students change gears or by introducing controversial content and asking students ponder it in a different way.

THE ROLE OF THE TEACHER IN CASE-BASED LEARNING

The role of the teacher in a case-based learning classroom is going to look much different than in a traditional classroom setting.

The teacher's main tasks in providing the correct environment for learning in this manner include:

- introducing the case,
- discussing the main points and ethical dilemmas,
- conferencing with students,
- interrupting strategically,
- finding an authentic audience, and
- closing the case (reflection).

For most of these tasks, the teacher is not the engine of the learning—the students are. The teacher is instead managing the case and making sure it goes where the best learning can take place. Just like a driver's education car with the extra wheel, there are times when the teacher takes over and directs the learning, only to relent to the students once he has steered it in a more interesting path.

Introduction to the Case

The teacher can take a major role during an introduction to the case or do a lot of the behind-the-scenes planning and then provide material to the students. It depends on how familiar the students are with case-based learning as well as their age or ability. For a beginner class, the teacher might assume the sage on the stage role, explaining the basic ideas behind the case, including a summary and the major ideas. For a more experienced class, the teacher might just distribute a selected reading to the class without any direction other than to find the main arguments that might be debated. The understanding of the case and the breakdown of its central components come from the students and their analysis. You will need to determine how much of a role you want to play in introducing a case depending on your students and your own comfort level with case-based learning.

Discussion of the Main Points, Ethical Dilemmas

One role of the teacher is to lead or proctor a discussion to get ideas flowing and bring up different perspectives. Velenchik (2018) provided a general overview of this process:

> The discussion can take many forms, including closely directed questioning by faculty to help students draw out the information from the case and identify the central decisions or evaluations that need to be made, more open-ended questions and discussions as students evaluate options and weigh the evidence, and small group work by students focused on specific analytical tasks. Many faculty members use role-play as a technique to put students completely in the case environment. Ideally, case method discussions involve mostly conversation between and among students, rather than discussion centered on direct participation by the faculty member. Many case method teachers describe their role as conductor, facilitator, or guide, drawing attention to their role in setting up discussion in which students are the primary participants. (para. 5)

As you can see, the role of the teacher is not as traditional, but there has to be some involvement in guiding and fostering the discussion to produce the ideas and inspire students to really dig into the case.

Let us say that your class is conducting a case concerning global warming. Although 97% of scientists believe the Earth's climate is changing, a quarter of Americans are skeptical as to whether the climate is being affected or not. It would be interesting to have a discussion on this perspective. You could set up a discussion/debate in which you split the class in half. Half of your students must argue that global warming is happening, while the other half must take the stance that the climate is not being affected. As the teacher, you start the discussion with the following prompt: Is global warming a real thing?

Depending on the expertise of your class when it comes to having a discussion or on the topic, you can just let the students have at it, making a case for each of their sides, letting them feed off of one another. If they need a little nudge, allow them to use their devices to look up information to back their positions. If they need a big nudge, have prompt sheets that you randomly hand out to students with some facts about the topic. Students could use the information provided to pose arguments that will lead to further discussion.

Your goal as the teacher is not to be the voice of reason or the conveyor of knowledge and wisdom. Your main goal is to keep the discussion going. This means that when discussion slows down, you should pose an argument or question that will make students think. This might involve building some controversy. Your role should involve:

- asking open-ended questions so that students are not limited to a correct response,
- making neutral statements or questions as much as possible without taking sides in the discussion,
- posing "What if. . .?" scenarios for students to ponder,
- making controversial comments that will force students to take a side and form an opinion, and
- acting as the devil's advocate and discussing topics you may not agree with but will spark discussion.

Depending on how comfortable you are with coming up with discussion questions, you might want to prepare some questions ahead of time that you can refer to. This will mean trying to anticipate where the argument might go and identifying data and information that will spark even more discussion.

What Goes on While Students Work

While students are working on their case, the teacher's role shifts more to the guide from the side. This includes conferencing with students and having conversations about their approach to the case as well as how they are progressing. In this role, you want to give students space to work independently, but you also want to make sure you are constantly challenging them to think about things in a different way. There are typically three types of conferences you can have with students.

Status conferences. These conferences involve checking in with groups of students and making sure that they are progressing smoothly. You will likely provide a deadline for when the solution to the case is due, so the main purpose of these types of conferences is to ensure students are on track. Check in with groups to ensure all members can report on the status of what they are responsible for. You might find some group members right where they need to be while others seem to be struggling. You can work with these struggling students one-on-one and allow those whose progress is going as planned to work independently. Status conferences can be informal. You might even observe groups from afar to ascertain their progress. In some cases, you might only need to provide encouragement. It might be a good idea to schedule at least one formal status conference a week, preferably in the middle of the week, so that if students are struggling you can help get them back on track. During a status conference, allow students to do most of the talking.

Process conferences. These conferences involve reflection and looking at whether groups are producing high-quality products. Have groups present what they have done or are planning on doing, and then try to get them to think about ways to improve their work. These process conferences require you to be more involved in the conversation and to dig a little deeper than a status conference. Ensure that what students are producing is going to be valuable for their case. If students are spending the week conducting research, sit down with the group and look over the notes that were taken, what was learned from them, and how they can be applied to the solution of the case. Depending how long the project is, these conferences should be scheduled periodically with no more than a couple of weeks between each check-in. This gives students enough time to work independently and find what they need but also allows you and students to catch any potential issues before they get too problematic. Your level of input is up to your discretion, but ideally you should point out a couple of things for each group to think about and then have them use self-reflection skills to identify what their next steps will be to improve the case.

Design conferences. These conferences basically function as dress rehearsals before the final solution is presented in order to make sure issues are worked out and that groups are producing the highest quality products possible. There are a few ways these can work. The first way is by giving students the time to practice. That might mean dedicating an entire class to allow groups to share their solution with others and to get feedback. This might mean bringing in guest audiences, such as another class, to act as impartial evaluators who can offer feedback on the solution. Or groups within the class can swap the written solution to the case and conduct an evaluation using the rubric (if one is provided). A second way to conduct design conferences is to find a mentor who has an expertise and can offer meaningful advice to each group. If students are performing a mock trial, have them confer with a lawyer to offer advice and take a look at their solution. If students are studying a medical case, find doctors or nurses who can listen and offer advice as to whether students are developing realistic solutions. If groups are designing a product in science class, connect them with an engineer who can provide valuable insight. A third way to conduct design conferences is to film students' performances and then have them analyze their work. Seeing their presentation from a different vantage point might provide perspective and show where there are flaws or where improvements can be made. Your level of input is up to your discretion. You can act as an evaluator, providing feedback and advice for improvements. You might just point to items in the rubric (if there is one) for them to focus on making better. You might take a hands-off approach and leave it up to others to provide the advice. The more involved you are, however, the stronger students' solutions will be.

As you can see, while students are working, you need to pick and choose when it is and isn't valuable for you to be involved in students' progress. Part of the goal of case-based learning is to create self-sufficient learners. That means sometimes letting the groups figure out the case for themselves. Your main role should be finding ways to make students' case solutions better and getting students to go deeper into their work so that they are thinking critically about it rather than just repeating what someone else has done. Students should be actively creating.

Strategic Interruptions

In addition to the various conferences you might have with groups while they are working on their case, you should find opportunities to strategically interrupt. This means walking around the room or sitting in a strategic location where you can hear a lot of groups and eavesdrop on conversations. Do not wait to catch students getting off-task or to correct them when they are wrong. Wait for the opportunity to take an interesting thought or idea and help students explore it in depth.

An example opportunity would be if a group is mulling over a case concerning the death penalty. As the teacher, you can pose questions that will cause students to think about this issue in another way. Some of questions you might pose would be:

- How would you feel about this case if a member of your family or a close friend were the victim?
- What would you think about a person who is on death row, convicted with evidence that is circumstantial?

- What would be worse, the death penalty or spending the rest of your life in prison?
- Is capital punishment morally justified?
- What do you think about the fact that since 1973, 150 people on death row have been exonerated and released because of DNA evidence that showed them not to be guilty?
- What will happen if people know they can commit a murder and not get the death penalty for it?

Notice that none of these questions are black or white. Each involves an ethical gray area. The questions you pose should be open-ended as much as possible to challenge students' thinking. This does not mean you should try to change students' minds, but rather you should try to get them to consider all possibilities and perspectives. You might also get members of a group to form different opinions. This makes for lively discussion and debate within the group.

Interrupting strategically means becoming the meddler in the middle. According to McWilliam (2008), this means:

- less time giving instructions and more time spent being a usefully ignorant team member in the thick of the action
- less time spent being a custodial minimizer and more time spent being an experimenter, risk-taker and learner
- less time spent being a forensic classroom auditor and more time being a designer, editor and assembler
- less time spent being a counsellor and 'best buddy' and more time spent being a collaborative critic and authentic evaluator. (p. 88)

Your role as meddler in the middle will depend on your teaching style in general. If it is not something you are naturally comfortable with, it might take some time and effort to fill this role. It also might require some preparation ahead of time, generating questions beforehand.

Finding an Authentic Audience

Another role of the teacher during CBL is conducted behind the scenes, securing an authentic audience for your groups to present their solution to the case. Having an authentic audience can take a case to the next level. For example, Heath and Heath (2017) shared the story of a class at Hillsdale High School that accused William Golding, author of *Lord of the Flies*, of libeling human nature through the Trial of Human Nature. Students acted as either witnesses, lawyers, or judges as a part of the case. To up the ante, students were told they were going to present their case in a real courtroom. The teacher arranged for a bus to take the students to the local courthouse where he had gotten permission to use the courtroom. The jury was made up of the principal, superintendent, other teachers, and some parents. This made the case very real for the students. This authentic audience caused the learning to be more meaningful as evidenced by the fact that every student speech at graduation mentioned the trial.

You do not have to go to the extreme of taking students down to the courthouse, but if you are conducting a mock trial, you might make the classroom feel like an actual courtroom. Have a parent who is a lawyer sit in as the judge or bring in prominent members of the community to serve as the jury. Any of these would be easy to arrange and not cost you a cent.

Finding an authentic audience can require some effort and planning. At the beginning of the year, consider sending home or e-mailing a parent survey to see what expertise they might have that you could use to gather an authentic audience. Make relationships with local universities to see if there are professors or graduate students who would like to work with students. Reach out to small businesses in the community and use their expertise when it fits. Find ways to make what your students are doing matter more to them.

Closing the Case

The final role of the teacher is to guide students in the reflection of what they have learned. This is one of the most overlooked aspects of teaching. Often, teachers determine what students have learned using traditional assessments without asking them what they *really* learned. Reflection provides you with the opportunity to dive into what students have truly taken away from a learning experience. Sometimes a student's takeaway is not what you wanted him or her to learn, but understanding a student's experience is crucial.

CBL reflection involves providing students with an outlet for sharing what they learned about content, a skill, process, or themselves. This usually involves a protocol or a way to guide students through the reflection process. An example reflection protocol is the Fortune Cookie: Ask students to sum up in a single statement what they learned from the case. You can give them some slips of paper that look like fortunes and give students a few minutes to think of a response. A fortune should:

- be able to fit on a single slip,
- capture the main idea of what a student learned,
- be phrased like a fortune cookie (you might show students some examples), and
- impart wisdom.

Example student responses might include:

- Geometry can actually be used in the real world.
- You must learn to present before you can fly.
- Trying to do a recipe out of order just results in bad food.
- He who procrastinates doesn't always live to fight another day.

The Fortune Cookie protocol forces students to sum up their experiences in a very short statement. If you want students to be able to share more detail, you need to choose a protocol that allows for this. This could involve students journaling, pairing and sharing, creating a one-minute Flipgrid video of their thoughts, or using other outlets that give them room to share more. Your role is to match the protocol with the information you want to get out of students' reflections. If you want to understand students' feelings about a case, find a protocol that allows students to express them. Regardless of the results you want, it is important that you use a protocol. Without one, students might have difficulty focusing their reflection. This is especially true if your students have not experienced much reflection in the classroom.

Students' reflections do not need to be elaborate. You might consider just posing a prompt. For example, if students have been working on a case in which they dealt with a controversial topic, such as abortion, gay marriage, or the legalization of recreational drugs, you might give them an opportunity to process what their feelings are now that the case is over. You might introduce a prompt that allows students to privately reflect, typing it into an electronic journal that will only be for their eyes. The prompt might read: Have your opinions on this topic changed in any way? This prompt would allow someone who remains steadfast in his or her conviction to restate his or her feelings on the matter and to express why he or she still feels so strongly about it. Or if someone found his or her opinions influenced or changed by the case, he or she he could walk through how his or her views were affected.

If you are specifically reflecting on a process the students went through, such as learning how to make a podcast or create a WeVideo during the case, you might want to have a more public reflection. The prompt could be: Do you think this method of sharing what you learned was an effective one, or could there have been a better option? You want students to share this information because it will help you determine whether a similar or better product could be utilized in future cases. Rather than journaling privately, students might get into small groups and discuss the prompt, with you circulating around the room and gathering information that will help you to inform future lessons.

There are plenty of example protocols online, such as those provided by the School Reform Initiative, which can be found at https://www.schoolreforminitiative.org/protocols. Develop a stash of protocols that work well with your students and your style of teaching and use them when appropriate.

MAKING A CASE

The role of the teacher in a case-based learning environment is to guide students through the case but allow them to do most of the learning themselves. This is a role that takes some adjusting to if you are used to more traditional methods, but one that will allow your students to become self-sufficient, independent learners, rather than passive participants waiting for the teacher to give them what they are supposed to learn.

PART III

CASE STUDIES IN THE CONTENT AREAS

DOI: 10.4324/9781003233428-10

CHAPTER 7

CASE STUDIES IN MATHEMATICS

Story is such an integral part of case-based learning, but it might seem challenging to find a compelling story in math. This is because the best cases are usually open-ended with multiple possible answers, and math often involves seeking one answer. There is no shortage of stories in math, however. There are mathematicians who spend their entire careers studying a single math concept, such as Andrew Wiles, who spent 8 years working on the proof of Fermat's last theorem (Sexton, 2010). Could students study what such mathematicians could have done differently or somehow study how those mathematicians plan and think in order to solve problems? Students can benefit from learning about mathematicians, the struggle and perseverance it takes to solve complex problems, and how to think like real mathematicians. Consider films that tell the story behind the math, such as *The Imitation Game*, *A Beautiful Mind*, *The Man Who Knew Infinity*, and *Hidden Figures*. There are plenty of stories to be found in math—you might just have to dig deeply to find strong cases.

DOI: 10.4324/9781003233428-11

One strategy for finding the story in math is by linking the content to other subject areas. For instance, there tend to be stories in science, and there are many connections to math. Edward Kasner, an American mathematician, coined the term *googol*. This represents the number 1 followed by 100 zeroes (or 10^{100}). A googol is used primarily in sciences that involve very large numbers, such as biology, geology, chemistry, and astronomy. A case could center around the mathematical uses of that number and whether there is an easier way to represent these large numbers.

You can also find stories in the news that have math involved and build a case for checking its accuracy. A simple example might be this fictional article:

> With an estimated $127 million, *Captain Planet 4* proved a massive success, bringing in the third highest November opening of all time. The previous three films in the series had a 2.76 multiplier, which would suggest the fourth installment would finish around $350 million based on the film's domestic opening weekend.
>
> It is interesting to note exits, which show the film playing to an opening weekend crowd that was 55% male and 45% female. Additionally, 62% of the film's opening weekend crowd was age 25 or older.
>
> The international launch was 23% ahead of mega-hit *Space Zoo*. South Korea led the rest of the pack with $24.1 million, marking the highest March opening weekend ever, 18% ahead of *Space Zoo*. The UK generated $16.8 million, the third highest March launch for that market. Brazil opened with $13.4 million, representing the second best opening weekend of all-time, 52% ahead of *Space Zoo*.

Students could analyze this article: Is $127 with a multiplier of 2.76 really equal to $350 million, and does the past history of the other films truly show this? Students might have to determine numbers based on the math provided. If 55% of the audience was male and 45% female, what is the approximate number of each who went to see the movie? How does that compare to other recent films?

You can find stories in the news that have authentic outcomes, such as overpopulation, how math is leading to discoveries of new technology, or the geometry involved in famous structures and buildings and how this allows us to continue to make taller structures. You could develop real-world cases that are relevant to students, such as fundraising opportunities, city planning, or math in sports.

You can link math to history, whether it be in the math system developed by the Egyptians, the invention of the number zero by the Mesoamericans, or the math involved in such wonderful architecture as the Pyramids of Giza or the Coliseum. You can look at specific historical events that involve math, such as the following sample case, the stock market crash of 1929. In this case, students analyze what caused the market to drop, what numbers were involved, what could have happened if banks had better managed money, and other financial questions that can be solved with math. This is a case for older students and would work well in a math, social studies, or economics class.

SAMPLE CASE STUDY

Choosing a Topic

The stock market crash of 1929

Developing a Title

The Blackest of Tuesdays

Big Picture Questions to Ponder

- What were the major causes of the stock market crash of 1929?
- How did the crash affect the economy of the United States?
- Is there any way the crash could have been avoided?

Executive Summary

On Tuesday, October 29, 1929, billions of dollars were lost as investors traded 16 million shares at the New York Stock Exchange. At the sound of the opening bell, the market lost 12% of its value. From there, things just got worse. After 2 days, $30 billion had been lost. The wealthy became broke overnight. This caused panic amongst businesses that had to shut their doors because they could no longer afford to stay open. People went to the banks and demanded their money, but many banks had lost the money in the crash and thus had none to give, meaning people's money was just gone. This lack of confidence in the American economic system continued to cause problems.

What or Who Is Your Case Study About (Telling the Story)

This case is about the confidence the American people lost in the economy and how this led to a self-fulfilling prophecy. As people worried about the economy, they did not spend money. Businesses lost money and laid off their workforces, which then caused more businesses to fail, and so on and so forth, until a widespread economic downturn evolved. The key is finding when the public's confidence began to wane and determining ways to rebuild their confidence or prevent the crash from happening. What are strategies that could have been undertaken to maintain the public's confidence?

Problems That Were Faced

There were signs of a forthcoming crash, as the economy had gained strength over the preceding 9 years, and yet industry production was beginning to decline and unemployment was rising. As a result, stocks were valued at a much higher price than they were worth. In addition, with the rise of urbanization, there was a surplus of farming products, meaning they began to lose their value because of too much supply and not enough demand. The stock market crash was just a single event in the course of many that caused the economic downturn. There were attempts made to stymie the decline of the stock market. There were many investors, including the Rockefellers, who bought large amounts of stocks to show confidence in the economy and compel people to keep investing. The question that can be asked is: Were there other ways to prevent the crash and/or its aftereffects?

Your group must create a stock analysis in which you track the progress of major stocks that failed on Black Tuesday and determine if there was any way to prevent the crash. You must create a plan for how to resuscitate these stocks, as well as maintain the confidence of the American people in the economy.

Constraints of the Case

Students are required to:
- use the numbers and facts from the actual 1929 stock market,
- create a realistic mathematical model to predict how stocks would have performed with suggested changes made, and
- work within the theory of the economic cycle and what has caused other periods of bust and prosperity.

Research That Supports or Refutes the Case

Here are some sources that provide a picture of the economy at the time leading up to and during the stock market crash:
- "The Stock Market Crash of October 29, 1929," available at http://americainclass.org/sources/becomingmodern/prosperity/text4/colcommentarycrash.pdf
- "How to Build Your Own Trading Model in 8 Steps," available at https://www.thestreet.com/story/10414044/1/how-to-build-your-own-trading-model-in-8-steps.html
- "Build a Profitable Trading Model in 7 Easy Steps," available at https://www.investopedia.com/articles/active-trading/010614/build-profitable-trading-model-7-easy-steps.asp

■ "A Sectoral Analysis of the 1929 Stock Market Crash," available at https://scholarship.claremont.edu/cgi/viewcontent. cgi?referer=https://www.google.com/&httpsredir=1&arti cle=2555&context=cmc_theses

Outcome of the Actual Case for Discussion

The stock market crash of 1929 is one of the contributing factors to the Great Depression. The crash created a decade-long downturn of the economy, resulting in half of the banks failing and more than 15 million people becoming unemployed. Eventually, the economy rebounded. Some of the believed causes of the recovery were:

■ the cost of fighting World War II that increased manufacturing,

■ the reforms introduced by the New Deal,

■ the National Industrial Recovery Act of 1933,

■ the National Labor Relations Act of 1935,

■ international gold inflows,

■ raised confidence by a belief in President Franklin D. Roosevelt,

■ decreased unemployment as potential workers went off to war and died, and

■ fiscal policy innovations.

CHAPTER 8

CASE STUDIES IN LANGUAGE ARTS

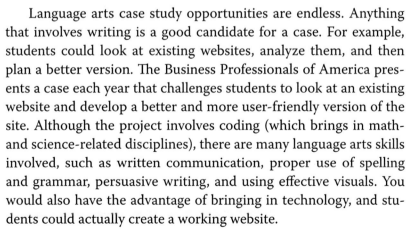

Language arts case study opportunities are endless. Anything that involves writing is a good candidate for a case. For example, students could look at existing websites, analyze them, and then plan a better version. The Business Professionals of America presents a case each year that challenges students to look at an existing website and develop a better and more user-friendly version of the site. Although the project involves coding (which brings in math- and science-related disciplines), there are many language arts skills involved, such as written communication, proper use of spelling and grammar, persuasive writing, and using effective visuals. You would also have the advantage of bringing in technology, and students could actually create a working website.

You could mix history and language arts. Students could use the Federalist and Anti-Federalist papers, the back and forth between those supporting the ratification of the Constitution and

 DOI: 10.4324/9781003233428-12

the nonsupporters. Students could read these collected essays and then produce their own version that either supports or opposes the Constitution, or write letters to the editor that analyze and evaluate these essays.

You could use books and their characters to make a case. An example of this would be taking the story of the Three Little Pigs and making a case against the Big Bad Wolf. Even though the story is simple, it could be made appropriate for older grade levels by adding more charges against the Big Bad Wolf. In the elementary classroom, he could be put on trial for destruction of property, at the middle school level he could also be charged with assault or attempted murder, and at the high school level he could be charged with terroristic threats. Students would have to use information from the story and real-world laws and legal precedents to construct their case. An example of this can be found at https://my edexpert.com/item/the-trial-of-the-big-bad-wolf. You could use any literary character or book to form a case around.

The case in this chapter takes the unfinished story of *The Mystery of Edwin Drood*, written by Charles Dickens and partially published in 1870, and asks students to complete it. This is a case for a higher grade level and would be ideal for British Literature classes. (*Note.* Depending on the level and ages of your students, you might just have them write a short ending that seems logical and fits with Dickens's writing style. For more advanced students, you might require that they create the 25 chapters that Dickens was unable to finish, using the original text as their guide when it comes to form, length, style, and tone. Students may also choose to use other performance assessments in order to present the story they have created, including but not limited to poems, movies, plays, spoken word performances, or graphic novels.)

SAMPLE CASE STUDY

Choosing a Topic

The Mystery of Edwin Drood by Charles Dickens

Developing a Title

Solving the Mystery of Edwin Drood

Big Picture Questions to Ponder

- Who is the murderer in the story?
- How do you think the book should have ended?
- Should someone's unfinished work be finished by someone else?

Executive Summary

The Mystery of Edwin Drood is the novel Charles Dickens was working on when he died in 1870. Dickens commonly published his books in serials. That meant a few chapters would come out, then the following month a few more chapters, and so on and so forth until the entire book had been published. This process could take several months to a year. He did this with *Edwin Drood*; however, he died with only six installments published, while five additional planned installments were left incomplete. As a result, the novel went unfinished. The book was a murder-mystery, and the person responsible for the murder was never revealed.

What or Who Is Your Case Study About (Telling the Story)

Your task is to read the original text of *The Mystery of Edwin Drood*, understanding essential literary and grammar conventions, such as tone, style, sentence structure, and mood. More importantly, your group will have to analyze and determine the themes of the unfinished book, specifically identifying timeless themes that still resonate today. Using this information, your team must finish the novel, determining who the murderer is and maintaining the timeless themes that your group identified. The difficulty in writing the ending is that you must develop the story and follow the tone and writing style that Dickens established in the first half, and the solution to the mystery must make some sense.

Problems That Were Faced

There are other authors who have tried to finish the novel. In 1870, an American author by the name of Robert Henry Newell attempted to complete it. However, he moved the story to the United States and did not follow the same tone as the original work. Henry Morford in 1872 serialized the ending, having Edwin Drood survive the murder attempt by Jasper. In 1873, Thomas Power James wrote the ending with the help of Charles Dickens himself. James purported to be channeling Dickens's spirit, although he was criticized heavily for including too many American mannerisms, and the solution to the mystery did not make much sense.

Constraints of the Case

Students are required to:
- keep the original storyline intact,
- not introduce new characters,
- keep the story in the time period and setting it was written in,
- write 25 chapters similar in length to the chapters Dickens wrote in his original, and
- complete the story in a logical way that makes sense.

Research That Supports or Refutes the Case

The group will need to read and study the original text by Charles Dickens. This will provide guidance on how to write the second half of the book. This will require an analysis of the original text. For a complete version of the text, visit https://en.wikisource.org/wiki/The_Mystery_of_Edwin_Drood.

Outcome of the Actual Case for Discussion

Although Dickens never completed the book, he did have an outline of the basic story, although he failed to name who the actual murderer was. The outline was published by John Forster, a friend of Dickens, in 1876 (as cited in Cox, 2006). Students can use this as a roadmap to the creation of their own ending. They are also more than welcome to read some of the other attempts to the ending. Although this story is more than 100 years old, you could use a variety of strategies to bring authenticity to the case, such as:

- having a public reading of the ending—either at a coffee house or in the classroom;
- inviting audience members to view the performance if students complete a performance assessment, such as a play or animated movie;
- inviting parents or other students to read the work and then post an Amazon-like review; or
- publishing the book in its entirety as an eBook that can be downloaded for free.

CHAPTER 9

CASE STUDIES IN SCIENCE

Scientists have to actively study cases, whether they are supporting a proposed theory, questioning scientific practices, testing a theory or hypothesis, or facing ethical dilemmas, such as cloning or stem cell research. Case-based learning is used quite often in the science of medicine. Doctors study past cases and try to do a better job or repeat a positive outcome. Experiment outcomes can also be studied. Can the experiment be repeated to result in the same outcome? Can improvements be made to the scientific method to have a better result? What can be learned from the mistakes the original case had?

Thus, there is no shortage of possible case study ideas in science. The National Center for Case Study Teaching in Science even has nearly 800 cases available on its website at http://sciencecases.lib. buffalo.edu/cs. In addition, there is usually a good story involving the science. Take, for instance, the development of penicillin. Al-

 DOI: 10.4324/9781003233428-13

exander Fleming discovered the antibiotic in 1928 when he noticed that a Petri dish had been mistakenly left out. It was contaminated by a blue-green mold from a nearby open window, which formed a halo of inhibited bacterial growth. From this, he concluded that the mold could be harnessed as an antibiotic. Almost as important, however, are the effects this discovery had on the medical field. The number of people died of infection lessened considerably as penicillin was used to treat it. What if penicillin had not been discovered by this accident . . . or what if it had been discovered earlier? Either question is an interesting way to approach the case.

The story of the invention of the light bulb is encased in the legend of Thomas Edison testing 1,000 different filaments before he settled on carbonized bamboo and changed the way the world lit its houses and streets. How about the creation of the airplane by Orville and Wilbur Wright? There were others who were working to be the first in flight. What about their prototypes did not work, and what changes could have been made to lead to greater success? This could also work as a math case study. Students might look at how some of the prototypes were built and what math concepts had to be mastered in order to achieve proper flight. Would some of these prototypes that did not work have revolutionized the way we think about flight had they flown successfully?

Science and its advancements also typically have a direct or indirect effect on people. When something is invented or new medical breakthroughs occur, people reap the benefits and changes. What might have happened had a breakthrough not occurred? For example, how would the world be different if the cell phone had not been developed? There are all sorts of possibilities.

The benefits of using case studies in science are many, including the fact that:

> Most science textbooks present decontextualized, or abstracted, knowledge. Cases, however, situate the knowledge in real-world contexts. Here, the cases provide the primary occasion for learn-

ing, rather than serve secondarily as illustrations or applications. (Allchin, 2013, p. 365)

You can draw from real-life cases, or you can edit and simplify the case to fit your academic needs. There are advantages and disadvantages to doing both. Real-life cases can be messy, making it difficult for students to sift through the information and find the most meaningful lessons or the content you intend to cover. Of course, this messiness can be a good thing, as life is often messy, making cases based on real life more authentic and teaching students how to negotiate a complex world.

A case that has been simulated or put into a "What if?" scenario can be more easily controlled and ensure that students are meeting the learning objectives you intend them to. However, simulated cases can sometimes feel artificial. If a student feels as though the case lacks authenticity, he or she might lose the motivation that comes with looking at relevant cases.

SAMPLE CASE STUDY

Choosing a Topic

The use of biogas as a renewable energy resource

Developing a Title

Cow Power

Big Picture Questions to Ponder

- How realistic are renewable energy sources in meeting the needs of energy consumers?
- How can we take the harmful effects of methane produced by cow manure and put it to use in energy conservation?
- What benefits would our community have by using a biogas digester in sustaining energy? How can this be done both efficiently and economically?

Executive Summary

A majority of energy that is consumed in the world is nonrenewable, whether it be coal, oil, or natural gas. This energy is consumed and can never be replaced. Not only that, the burning of these fossil fuels can cause damage to the environment through their pollution. Another harmful effect on the ozone comes from the amount of methane gas that comes from cows. Worldwide there are 1.5 billion cows with each one releasing an average of 100 kg of methane a year. According to the Food and Agriculture Organization of the United Nations (2006), "the livestock sector generates more greenhouse gas emissions as measured in CO2 equivalent—18 percent— than transport" (para. 2). What if we could create renewable energy sources and cut down on the amount of methane that is released by cows and their manure? It can be done with what is known as biogas.

Biogas uses cow manure, sewage, and other fecal matter and, through a device known as a digester, is able to convert this into energy. Because there is an unlimited amount of these materials, biogas is a renewable resource. In addition, waste materials that would otherwise pollute landfills or require the use of toxic chemicals in treatment plants, are treated on site and thus save money, energy, and materials. The use of biogas is used on different scales, as small as a home digester that produces energy for a single household, to countries such as China taking initiatives to make agriculture more efficient by installing more than 26.5 million biogas plants, which provide an output of 248 billion m³.

What or Who Is Your Case Study About (Telling the Story)

There are several stories about different countries using biogas in various ways, but this case will focus on Sweden. The country is trying to determine how biogas can allow it to develop a net-zero emission economy by the year 2045 (Bioenergy International, 2018). In order to do this, Sweden has to increase its number of biogas plants to nearly 300. There are government initiatives to increase the amount of TWh (terawatt hours) of biogas to 15 by the year 2030. The country is beginning to use biogas for heating, electricity, and even fuel for vehicles. Rather than just focusing on farms, Sweden has used sewer water treatment plants, landfills, codigestion plants, and industrial facilities. As a result, 64% of the sold volumes of vehicle gas was ungraded biogas, the highest percentage of any country (Swedish Energy Agency, 2011). This is one way that an entire country's government decided to take on the challenge of creating more renewable energy through the use of biogas.

You will investigate different countries to see how people are using this form of energy locally as well as nationally. You must then determine what would realistically be the best way to bring biogas to your own community. Would it be mandated by the government, be a more grassroots approach with individuals choosing to implement biogas, or a combination of strategies? You need to determine on what scale biogas energy will be used, whether it is household, small scale, medium scale, or large scale.

Problems That Were Faced

The major problem with renewable energy, in general, is convincing people to change over from fossil fuels. This is for a variety of reasons. One reason is fossil fuels produce quite a bit more energy than renewable sources. Renewable energy can be inefficient and, thus, unreliable because we cannot always control when we receive it and how much we receive. Probably the biggest problem would be cost. A lot of renewable energy sources, biogas included, depend on the technology it takes to convert material to energy. This technology can be expensive to purchase and to maintain. Coal, on the other hand, is quite cheap to mine and convert to energy. You simply have to burn it. One of the challenges of this case is finding cheap and efficient ways to use biogas. This also involves helping people to see the value in using such an energy source and what the overall benefits to them would be.

Constraints of the Case

Students are required to consider how:
- a biogas digester costs money and needs an infrastructure to provide energy output,
- the production of biogas creates as much air pollution as is produced by natural gas consumption, and
- the amount of farmland a community has or the willingness of its government to provide the infrastructure needed to produce energy from biogas.

Research That Supports or Refutes the Case

Some helpful research sources follow:

- Video: "How Does a Biogas Plant Work?" available at https://www.youtube.com/watch?v=3UafRz3QeO8
- Video: "The Science of Biogas," available at https://www.youtube.com/watch?v=HsPe88lYFE8
- Video: "Biogas Digester What You Need to Know," available at https://www.youtube.com/watch?v=BNH01N7XPC4
- Video: "Biogas Final Compressed," available at https://www.youtube.com/watch?v=4AUczCL3nok
- "Biogas in Sweden: The Answer to Deeper Decarbonisation?" available at https://bioenergyinternational.com/opinion-commentary/biogas-in-sweden-the-answer-to-deeper-decarbonisation
- Video: "Biogas Production in Kenya Part 1-Urban Farmer," available at https://www.youtube.com/watch?v=v6VYsU-vpKa0
- Video: "Biogas Production in India, From Cow Poop!" available at https://www.youtube.com/watch?v=RMrRv_B2NL4
- "Biogas Digesters at the Community of Tamera in Portugal | Renewable Energy | Auroras Eye Films," available at https://www.youtube.com/watch?v=cabw8enOC8Q
- "Low Cost Plastic Drum Biogas in the Philippines," available at https://www.youtube.com/watch?v=gIZTpTmSHRQ

Outcome of the Actual Case for Discussion

What the future holds for biogas has yet to be determined. One would like to think that with countries such as China, Germany, and India getting their governments involved in the production of biogas, other countries would get on board. As of 2017, the world was using 352,780 GWh a year. This seems like a lot, but in the overall energy production scale, biogas represents only 10% of the overall energy consumed, with coal, natural gas, and oil consisting of 80%. The good news is that there is an upward trend of biogas use. In 1990, use was less than 50,000 GWh.

CHAPTER 10

CASE STUDIES IN SOCIAL STUDIES

Social studies is rife with topics and historical figures that can be utilized for case studies. Because social studies encompasses government, the court system, psychology, citizenship, social responsibility, and sociology, there is an abundance of cases that can be formed.

There are many historical events that students can study, including making a case for whether our Founding Fathers should have chosen a president or a monarch and what might have happened, or studying the seven wonders of the ancient world and determining whether they all belonged on the list and if there were other ancient structures that deserved the honor more.

You could use historical figures. Aaron Burr, infamous for shooting and killing Alexander Hamilton, also was involved in a couple of other political scandals, such as not relenting the election to Thomas Jefferson even when it seemed obvious that those

DOI: 10.4324/9781003233428-14

who voted for him intended for Burr to be Vice President, or when he was accused of treason for offering to help the Spaniards overthrow the U.S. government. Students could conduct a case study to analyze whether Burr would have made a good president or not and how things might have been different. You could have students review the court case of Joan of Arc and determine whether she was a tragic hero or just plain insane.

Another option is local issues, such as looking at the city's curfew laws and seeing if there is enough evidence to justify them or whether there could be a compelling argument for expanding the laws or studying whether the school's recycling program is doing any good for the environment. The class could even look at the ethics of social media and determine whether it is a useful or harmful method of communicating.

History can also be combined with other subject areas to make a case. If you want to teach the scientific principal of evolution, your class could analyze the Scopes Monkey Trial and consider retrying the case. For math, you could look at the School of Pythagoras, an ancient Greek cult that discovered irrational numbers and then, concerned about the ramifications of its discovery, sought to keep it secret from society. Language arts could find your class looking at the works of William Shakespeare and trying to determine whether he is indeed the author of the great works he is attributed to.

The topic in this chapter's case is the trial of Socrates, the famous Greek philosopher. This is a topic that is rife with teachable moments. Issues addressed include:

- freedom of speech,
- the death penalty,
- the meaning of citizenship,
- how the government should deal with agitators, and
- whether youth can be corrupted through education.

This is a unique case because not only are students going to be required to learn about the history of Socrates and why he was persecuted, but also the trial will be held in an American court system so students will have to be familiar with how that works and what amendments to the Constitution come into play.

This case is designed for middle school students, although it can be adapted to be used with high school students. One way to do that is by having students read Plato's *Apology*, which is the defense that Socrates supposedly made at his trial. A version of it can be accessed here: http://classics.mit.edu/Plato/apology.html.

SAMPLE CASE STUDY

Choosing a Topic

The death of Socrates

Developing a Title

The Price of Freedom and Citizenship

Big Picture Questions to Ponder

- Were Socrates's crimes serious enough to deem punishable by death?
- Is there a limitation to what can be taught?

■ What would have happened if Socrates were tried in a present-day U.S. court?

Executive Summary

In 399 BC, the Greek philosopher Socrates was put on trial for the crimes of defying the gods, corrupting the youth, and trying to overthrow the government. The penalty for being found guilty was death. He had to fight for his life in the Athenian court system in which the number of jurors depended on who showed up. More than 500 people served as his jury.

What or Who Is Your Case Study About (Telling the Story)

The case revolves around Socrates, a famous Greek philosopher who is considered the father of moral philosophy. He was the teacher of many other famous philosophers, such as Plato, Xenophon, and Antisthenes. Ironically, he was accused of corrupting youngsters by encouraging them to think and go against the status quo. Socrates devoted his life to questioning. He was known as the creator of the Socratic Method, which involved an instructor breaking down a large philosophical issue and asking questions until the answers provided eventually reveal a truth. The Socratic Method was considered to be the defining element of the American legal system in which lawyers ask questions of witnesses with the motive at getting at the truth.

Problems That Were Faced

This trial is going to be conducted in an American courtroom, meaning there are many problems to consider in addition to the accusations against Socrates. The prosecution is seeking the death penalty or capital punishment. But according to the Eighth Amendment, there is no cruel and unusual punishment. Do Socrates's crimes necessitate the death penalty, or is there a punishment that better suits the charges? In addition, if this is a U.S. legal system, we have the First Amendment, which is the freedom of speech. Was Socrates within his legal right to question the government, or is his corruption of the youth an instance where this crosses the line?

Constraints of the Case

Students are required to:
■ research and prepare for the trial,
■ use the proceedings of the American court system, and
■ utilize the facts of the case from ancient Greece (even though Socrates is being tried in present day).

Research That Supports or Refutes the Case

For a middle school class, resources include *The Trial of Socrates* by I. F. Stone. From a resource such as this, students can learn who acted as witnesses, what they testified about, and other details to make a case for or against Socrates. For more advanced classes, students might actually read Plato's *Apology*, which includes the speech

Socrates gave at his trial. Students could then determine a better defense that he could have made in order to be found not guilty. That text can be found here: http://classics.mit.edu/Plato/apology.html.

In order to make the case accessible for middle school students, the research can be scaffolded to provide students with a case overview, such as the one in Table 2, which lays out the various roles and duties students will have to play in the mock trial.

Outcome of the Actual Case for Discussion

Socrates was found guilty of the offenses he was accused of. As punishment, he was forced to drink hemlock, which killed him. There are many who feel that Socrates was a scapegoat for the political turmoil that was going on at the time because the Spartans were defeated in the Peloponnesian war. Because the Athenians were trying to start a new type of government called democracy, any voices that opposed the government needed to be silenced. Socrates was one of those voices. There are some historians who argue that Socrates, in effect, committed suicide, making himself a martyr. The reason for this is that his execution was delayed for 30 days due to a religious festival, and many of his students made attempts to help him escape, but he refused. The arguments made for his not wanting to escape were:

1. He believed such a flight would indicate a fear of death, which he believed no true philosopher has.
2. If he fled Athens, his teaching would fare no better in another country, as he would continue questioning all he met and undoubtedly incur others' displeasure.
3. Having knowingly agreed to live under the city's laws, he implicitly subjected himself to the possibility of being accused of crimes by its citizens and judged guilty by its jury.

Table 2

Trial of Socrates Case Overview Outline

Role	Tasks
Judge	• The judge is the chief executive of the courtroom. Providing justice is the most critical duty of the judge—to see that people are treated correctly and fairly according to the law. • In Athens, judges were referred to as magistrates, but they did not sit on court cases. Instead, the Council of Citizens acted as both judge and jury. We are going to try Socrates using a U.S. court system to teach you how it works, so we will be using a judge. • The judge will be coached by the teacher as to how to run the courtroom and then required to complete the judge's packet. • The judge's job in this activity is one of the most important. He or she must control the pace of the court case and must keep things moving along.
Prosecutor	• The prosecutor represents the victims of the crime. It is his or her duty to protect society and individual victims. • In Athens, anyone could bring an accusation against another citizen. Whoever made the accusation was then responsible for trying to prove the guilt of that person. • In the United States, lawyers do this for the victims. No case may exist without a victim. They are the reason for having all of the other actors present in court. The victim is the person who is pursuing the lawsuit. • The victims in our case are Meletus, Anytus, and Lycon, the same people prosecuting the case. In Athens, the victims who brought the case to light also had to prosecute the case. In the U.S., you hire a lawyer to present your case for you—someone who knows the laws and is aware of all of your rights. • The members of the prosecution must interview their five witnesses and understand what questions they are going to ask their witnesses. They also will want to prepare their opening statement and closing argument as well as possible cross-examination questions.

141

Table 2, continued.

Role	Tasks
Defense	• On the opposite side of the argument is the defense attorney. This person represents the citizen accused of the crime. The defense attorney ideally helps a person from the time of his or her arrest throughout the trial process. • In Athens, you had to defend yourself. So Socrates had to defend himself against the accusations of his enemies. • Here in the U.S., there is a saying that "he who represents himself is a fool." Lawyers usually defend the case for the accused. In fact, according to law, a lawyer must be provided, even if the person cannot afford one. • The defense lawyers in our case are going to be three of Socrates's students—Aristotle, Plato, and Euclid. • The members of the defense must interview their five witnesses and understand what questions they are going to ask their witnesses. They also will want to prepare their opening statement and closing argument as well as possible cross-examination questions.
Character and Expert Witnesses	• All trials have witnesses to make the case either stronger or weaker, depending on which side presents the witness. • The prosecution would want to present witnesses that make its case stronger, while the defense would present witnesses to counter the prosecution's arguments or weaken its case. • There are two types of witnesses—expert and character. • An expert witness will testify about an area in which he or she has a specialized skill. Some examples are fingerprinting, handwriting analysis, and psychiatric evaluation. • A character witness is also known as a lay witness. Character witnesses are usually permitted to speak about non-specific issues in court and are there to give examples as to why the defendant is either guilty or innocent, based on their observation of events rather than any expertise. They also can speak to the reputation of people on trial and show either how they are good people or how they are susceptible to committing the crime they are accused of. • We need 10 witnesses—four expert and six character. • The witnesses must read their character profile and answer questions as their characters would, not themselves. They must be interviewed by one of the three lawyers. Each witness must answer at least three questions. There can be more but no less.

Table 2, continued.

Role	Tasks
Jury	• Jurors are the people who decide whether the accused is guilty or not guilty. They are supposed to be impartial to the case or aspects of it. For example, if the prosecution is seeking the death penalty for a crime, it would not have someone on the jury who is opposed to the death penalty. Or if the person on trial is Hispanic, you wouldn't want someone on the jury who is racist toward Hispanics. • In the U.S., juries are made up of 12 people who are regular citizens with regular jobs and are called to jury duty by the state. • Almost everyone in their adult life will be called to jury duty. It is considered to be part of your duty as a citizen. • The jurors must vote unanimously for either guilty or not guilty. If they cannot all decide the same verdict, it is known as a hung jury and the defendant goes free. Usually when this happens, though, the case will be retried with another jury. But once a person is found not guilty, he or she cannot be retried for the same case twice. This is known as double jeopardy. • In Greece, things worked differently. The jury was made up more than 500 people who volunteered to be the jury. They acted not only as jury but also as judge. • Everyone who does not have a part in the trial will be on the jury.

CASE STUDIES AND CASE-BASED LEARNING

Table 2, continued.

Role	Tasks
Socrates	• Socrates is the accused in the trial. He is a wise man of Athens and considered one of the most important philosophers of his time. He has been spreading his teachings in the marketplace, mostly to the sons of the rich and influential. This, in addition to his bad habit of pointing out people's flaws, most of whom are powerful politicians, has made Socrates a lot of enemies. He has made enemies of the politicians represented by Anytus, the poets represented by Meletus, and the artisans represented by Lycon.
	• At the same time, Socrates is also greatly admired by others for his willingness to explore an argument wherever it might lead. Some of his admirers are the three defense lawyers, Plato, Aristotle, and Euclid.
	• Socrates spends most of his time in the marketplace conversing about ethical issues. Although a stone-cutter by trade, he stopped doing this in favor of spreading his ideas.
	• In addition to the charge of corrupting the youth, Socrates has been accused of being associated with an undemocratic faction known as the sophists, an accusation Socrates denies.
	• Socrates is a very vain man, thinking that no one is more intelligent than he. He has also claimed throughout his life to hear voices, which he interprets as signs from the gods.
	• Socrates must aid the defense lawyers in interviews and prepare his own defense when he gets up on the stand. He must write at least three questions the defense team will ask him during the trial.
	• Socrates will waive his Fifth Amendment right to not testify against himself, taking the stand in this case.

144

To do otherwise would have caused him to break his "social contract" with the state, and so harm the state, an unprincipled act.

4. If he escaped at the instigation of his friends, then his friends would become liable in law (Weiss, 1998).

The legacy and teachings of Socrates live on though, mostly in the writings of one of his most famous pupils, Plato. Plato wrote several pieces that espoused the philosophies of Socrates, which are still studied and used today including *Apology*, the defense that Socrates made at his trial.

CONCLUSION

MAKING A
FINAL CASE

This book has outlined the merits of case-based learning and what it can do for your students. Let us look at one final case.

Choosing a Topic

The engagement of students

Developing a Title

How Do I Engage My Students?

DOI: 10.4324/9781003233428-15

Big Picture Questions to Ponder

- How does a teacher engage students who no longer find school inspiring?
- How do students gain an enduring understanding of what they are learning?
- How do schools create self-sufficient, lifelong learners?

Executive Summary

A teacher named Steve is tasked with teaching his class about U.S. government. He has been teaching this unit for several years but just has not gotten the level of student engagement he would like. Students all seem to get the basics of government, but they are not seemingly excited about the prospect of how the government can work for them, nor do they understand the context of how it can be used. There are many students, who weeks after the unit, cannot seem to remember what they learned about government. This frustrates Steve. He wants to find a way to teach his students about the U.S. government but, at the same time, get them excited about it.

What or Who Is Your Case Study About (Telling the Story)

This case is about several people. First off, it is about Steve and his desire to engage his students. He is at least willing to try something different, knowing that the definition of insanity is doing the same thing over and over and expecting a different result. He wants to get different results and knows that the only way to do this is to do something in the classroom. This case is also about the students and the fact that they come to school because they know they have to, not because they want to. They love to learn, but they do not like to learn the way schools and teachers are expecting them to. They are itching to be involved and be a part of the learning process. This case is also about the school that tries to support teachers as best it can with resources and professional development, but ultimately is evaluated on its success by the scores of the students on state-mandated testing.

Problems That Were Faced

- The hesitancy of the teacher to try something new and outside of his comfort zone.
- The reluctance of the students who are not keen on working collaboratively in groups due to past issues.
- The fear of administration that might frown upon innovative learning that could affect test scores.

Constraints of the Case

The constraints include:
- content standards that are part of the curriculum have to be covered in the class;
- time, in that the teacher only has so much of it; and
- the ability of the students to attempt to work with others collaboratively.

Research That Supports or Refutes the Case

Steve considers three different strategies.

- **Strategy #1:** Steve lectures to students about the characteristics and merits of the U.S. government. Students get supplemental materials by watching online videos and reading excerpts of *Democracy in America* by Alexis de Tocqueville. Students will then take a written exam in which they must talk about the characteristics and merits of the U.S. government.

- **Strategy #2:** Steve divides students into teams and has each of them research a different government, such as communist China, the monarchy of England, the dictatorship of Cuba, and the U.S. government. Groups are asked to make an argument for the effectiveness of government they studied in a class debate.

- **Strategy #3:** Steve asks students to study the Articles of Confederation, the first document that governed our country, determining all of the problems and issues with it. Rather than throwing it out as our forefathers did, groups are tasked with writing a revised Articles of Confederation that fixes many of the issues and would allow for the country to be able to function. Students will write up this document and present it to city council.

Outcome of the Actual Case for Discussion

Which strategy would you choose? The outcome of this case will actually be written by you and the decisions you make. Hopefully you select the third option, which is case-based learning.

As a final reminder, when implementing case-based learning it is best to remember the following (Poorvu Center for Teaching and Learning, 2019):

- **Take baby steps if new to CBL:** While entire courses and curricula may involve case-based learning, instructors who desire to implement on a smaller-scale can integrate a single case into their class, and increase the number of cases utilized over time as desired.

- **Use cases in classes that are small, medium or large:** Cases can be scaled to any course size. In large classes with stadium seating, students can work with peers nearby, while in small classes with more flexible seating arrangements, teams can move their chairs closer together. CBL can introduce more noise (and energy) in the classroom to which an instructor often quickly becomes accustomed. Further, students can be asked to work on cases outside of class, and wrap up discussion during the next class meeting.

- **Encourage collaborative work:** Cases present an opportunity for students to work together to solve cases which the historical literature supports as beneficial to student learning (Bruffee, 1993). Allow students to work in groups to answer case questions.

- **Form diverse teams as feasible:** When students work within diverse teams, they can be exposed to a variety of perspectives that can help them solve the case. Depending on the context of the course, priorities, and the background information gathered about the students enrolled in the class, instructors may choose to organize student groups to allow for diversity in factors such as current course grades, gender, race/ethnicity, personality, among other items.

- **Use stable teams as appropriate:** If CBL is a large component of the course, a research-supported practice is to keep teams together long enough to go through the stages of group development: forming, storming, norming, performing and adjourning (Tuckman, 1965).

- **Walk around to guide groups:** In CBL instructors serve as facilitators of student learning. Walking around allows the instructor to monitor student progress as well as identify and support any groups that may be struggling. Teaching assistants can also play a valuable role in supporting groups.
- **Interrupt strategically:** Only every so often, for conversation in large group discussion of the case, especially when students appear confused on key concepts. An effective practice to help students meet case learning goals is to guide them as a whole group when the class is ready. This may include selecting a few student groups to present answers to discussion questions to the entire class, asking the class a question relevant to the case using polling software, and/or performing a mini-lesson on an area that appears to be confusing among students.
- **Assess student learning in multiple ways:** Students can be assessed informally by asking groups to report back answers to various case questions. This practice also helps students stay on task, and keeps them accountable. Cases can also be included on exams using related scenarios where students are asked to apply their knowledge. (sec. 3)

By using this method of teaching, you will be bringing the real world to students and, more importantly, providing context for where what they are learning fits. Let us take a look at the four cases in this book and how you can make them even more authentic:

- **The Blackest of Tuesdays:** When students turn in their final portfolio, it will be analyzed and scrutinized by people who work with stocks for a living or bankers.
- **Solving the Mystery of Edwin Drood:** Have students take their finished novel and self-publish it on Amazon Kindle. This way it will be available for parents and the public to download and read.

- **Cow Power:** The plans that groups come up with could be presented to city council or presented to environmental scientists.
- **The Price of Freedom and Citizenship:** You could livestream the case like Court TV. Then invite parents to watch the proceedings or upload the video to YouTube.

This brings relevance to what students are doing and makes them actually care about why they are learning it. Is that not what we want for all of our students?

REFERENCES

Allchin, D. (2013). Problem- and case-based learning in science: An introduction to distinctions, values, and outcomes. *CBE—Life Sciences Education, 12*, 364–372.

Barrows, H., & Tamblyn, R. (1980). *Problem-based learning: An approach to medical education.* New York, NY: Springer.

Bioenergy International. (2018). *Biogas in Sweden: The answer to deeper decarbonisation?* Retrieved from https://bioenergyinter national.com/opinion-commentary/biogas-in-sweden-the-an swer-to-deeper-decarbonisation

Bloom, B. (Ed.). (1956). *Taxonomy of educational objectives: The classification of educational goals. Handbook I: Cognitive domain.* New York, NY: Longmans Green.

Bruffee, K. S. (1993). *Collaborative learning: Higher education, interdependence, and authority of knowledge.* Baltimore, MD: Johns Hopkins University Press.

Center for Innovation in Teaching and Learning. (2019). The case method. *University of Illinois.* Retrieved from https://citl.illi nois.edu/citl-101/teaching-learning/resources/teaching-strate gies/the-case-method

Centre for Teaching and Learning. (n.d.). What is case-based learning? *Queen's University*. Retrieved from https://www.queensu.ca/ctl/teaching-support/instructional-strategies/case-based-learning

Cox, A. J. (2006). The "Drood" remains revisited: "First fancy." *Dickens Quarterly, 23,* 108.

Curtin Learning and Teaching. (2015). *Authentic learning.* Retrieved from https://clt.curtin.edu.au/teaching_learning_practice/student_centred/authentic.cfm

Doyle, A. (2019). How often do people change jobs? *The Balance Careers.* Retrieved from https://www.thebalancecareers.com/how-often-do-people-change-jobs-2060467

Dunne, D., & Brooks, K. (2004). *Teaching with cases* (Green Guide No. 5). Halifax, NS: Society for Teaching and Learning in Higher Education.

EduTech Wiki. (2018). *Case-based learning.* Retrieved from http://edutechwiki.unige.ch/en/Case-based_learning

Engineering is Elementary. (2019). *The engineering design process.* Retrieved from https://www.eie.org/overview/engineering-design-process

Ertmer, P. A., & Russell, J. D. (1995). Using case studies to enhance instructional design education. *Educational Technology, 35*(4), 23–31.

Food and Agriculture Organization of the United Nations. (2006). *Livestock a major threat to environment.* Retrieved from http://www.fao.org/newsroom/en/news/2006/1000448/index.html

Garvin, D. A. (2003). Making the case: Professional education for the world of practice. *Harvard Magazine.* Retrieved from http://harvardmagazine.com/2003/09/making-the-case-html

Gwenna Moss Centre for Teaching and Learning. (2017). Case-based learning: Providing a context for abstract material. *University of Saskatchewan.* Retrieved from https://teaching.usask.ca/articles/case-based-learning.php

Har, K. B. (2013). Authentic learning. *The Hong Kong Institute of Education.* Retrieved from https://www.eduhk.hk/aclass/Theories/AuthenticLearning_28June.pdf

Heath, C., & Heath, D. (2017). *The power of moments: Why certain experiences have extraordinary impact.* New York, NY: Simon & Schuster.

Ireland, C. (2015). The makeover of Mexico City. *The Harvard Gazette.* Retrieved from https://news.harvard.edu/gazette/story/2015/02/the-makeover-of-mexico-city

Lynn, L. E. (1999). *Teaching and learning with cases: A guidebook.* Chappaqua, NY: Seven Bridges Press.

MacGregor, H. (2015). La Paz's cable-car system Teleferico a heady ride that bridges Bolivia's values. *Los Angeles Times.* Retrieved from https://www.latimes.com/travel/la-tr-d-bolivia-teleferico-20151213-story.html

McWilliam, E. (2008). *The creative workforce: How to launch young people into high-flying futures.* Sydney, Australia: University of New South Wales Press.

MESA. (n.d.). The engineering design process. *University of Southern California.* Retrieved from https://zk98i2roxgh3cydvu191ilcg-wpengine.netdna-ssl.com/wp-content/uploads/2018/08/The-Engineering-Design-Process.pdf

Mostert, M. P. (2007). Challenges of case-based teaching. *The Behavior Analyst Today, 8,* 434–440.

Mullins, G. (1994). The evaluation of teaching in a problem-based learning context. In S. E. Chen, R. Cowdroy, A. Kingsland, & M. Ostwald (Eds.), *Reflections on problem based learning* (pp. 105–124). Sydney: Australian Problem Based Learning Network.

National Research Council. (2011). *Promising practices in undergraduate science, technology, engineering, and mathematics education: Summary of two workshops.* Washington, DC: The National Academies Press. https://doi.org/10.17226/1309

Nield, D. (2016). Singapore just launched a plan to fill the city with 3D-printed homes. *Science Alert.* Retrieved from https://www.sciencealert.com/singapore-is-planning-on-building-3d-printed-homes-for-its-people

Nova Education. (2015). *This scientist learned by doing science and your students can too.* Retrieved from https://www.pbs.org/

wgbh/nova/article/this-scientist-learned-by-doing-science-and-your-students-can-too

Poorvu Center for Teaching and Learning. (2019). Case-based learning. *Yale*. Retrieved from https://poorvucenter.yale.edu/faculty-resources/strategies-teaching/case-based-learning

Reeves, T. C., Herrington, J., & Oliver, R. (2002). Authentic activities and online learning. In *Quality Conversations, Proceedings of the 25th HERDSA Annual Conference* (p. 562). Perth, Western Australia: Higher Education Research and Development Society of Australasia.

Schommer, M. (1990). Effects of belief about the nature of knowledge on comprehension. *Journal of Educational Psychology, 82*, 498–504.

Sexton, M. R. (2010). Top 10 greatest mathematicians. *Listverse*. Retrieved from http://listverse.com/2010/12/07/top-10-greatest-mathematicians

The Staff of the Princeton Review. (2019). What is law school like: First-year curriculum. *The Princeton Review*. Retrieved from https://www.princetonreview.com/law-school-advice/first-year-curriculum

Stanley, T. (2018). *Authentic learning: Real-world experiences that build 21st-century skills*. Waco, TX: Prufrock Press.

Swedish Energy Agency. (2011). *Biogas in Sweden*. Retrieved from https://energimyndigheten.a-w2m.se/Home.mvc?ResourceId=2569

Thistlethwaite, J. E., Davies, D., Ekeocha, S., Kidd, J. M., MacDougall, C., Matthews, P. (2012). The effectiveness of case-based learning in health professional education. A BEME systematic review: BEME Guide No. 23. *Medical Teacher, 34*, e421–e444.

Vander Ark, T. (2013). CEOs want hard-working decision-making team players. *Getting Smart*. Retrieved from https://www.gettingsmart.com/2013/05/ceos-want-hard-working-decision-making-team-players

Velenchik, A. (2018). Teaching with the case method. *Pedagogy in Action: The SERC Portal for Educators.* Retrieved from https://serc.carleton.edu/sp/library/cases/index.html

Wagner, T. (2008). *The global achievement gap: Why even our best schools don't teach the new survival skills our children need—and what we can do about it.* New York, NY: Basic Books.

Wagner, T. (2012). *Creating innovators: The making of young people who will change the world.* New York, NY: Scribner.

Weiss, R. (1998). *Socrates dissatisfied: An analysis of Plato's Crito.* Oxford, England: Oxford University Press.

Williams, B. (2005). Case based learning—a review of the literature: is there scope for this educational paradigm in prehospital education? *Emergency Medical Journal, 22,* 577–581.

Zoltan, I. (2019). Ignaz Semmelweis: German-Hungarian physician. *Encyclopedia Britannica.* Retrieved from https://www.britannica.com/biography/Ignaz-Semmelweis

ABOUT THE AUTHOR

Todd Stanley is the author of many teacher education books, including *Project-Based Learning for Gifted Students: A Handbook for the 21st-Century Classroom, Using Rubrics for Performance-Based Assessment: A Practical Guide to Evaluating Student Work*, and the *10 Performance-Based STEM Projects* series. He was a classroom teacher for 18 years, teaching students as young as second graders and as old as high school seniors, and was a National Board Certified teacher. He is currently gifted services coordinator for Pickerington Local School District, OH, where he lives with his wife, Nicki, and two daughters, Anna and Abby. You can follow him on Twitter @the_gifted_guy, or you can visit his website at https://www.thegift edguy.com, which features blogs, video tutorials, free resources, and a library of cases.